SACRED HEALING

A Guide to Awakening, Feeling, and Living Your Best Life

by Kimberly Weimer, LCSW

Copyright ©2025 *Kimberly Weimer*
All Rights Reserved.

DEDICATION

To my greatest teachers, my deepest loves—Hunter and Tyler.

You are the reason I rose.
The reason I healed.
The reason I broke every chain I was born into.

Tyler, your strength, loyalty, and heart have shaped you into the kind of man this world so deeply needs. Watching you love with integrity and lead with compassion fills me with awe.

Hunter, your resilience, wisdom, and kindness reveal a soul far beyond your years. You've faced loss with grace and turned pain into power.

You are the cycle-breakers.
You are the hope I once only dreamed of.
Because of you, I became more.

May this book be a reflection of the healing we've done together— and a reminder that you can be anything, do anything, and love without limits.

You are, and will always be, the best thing I ever created.

ACKNOWLEDGMENTS

To my sons, Hunter and Tyler—
You were the reason I chose to heal. I wanted to be the best mother I could be, and that meant breaking cycles of pain I was born into. Watching you grow into kind, honorable, and emotionally intelligent men has been the greatest reward of my life. You have each broken generational curses with strength and grace. Hunter, thank you for being my biggest cheerleader—for encouraging me to follow my dreams, start my business, share my voice, and write this book. Your belief in me carried me forward more than you know.

To Spirit—
Thank you for trusting me with this divine calling. Thank you for never letting me hide from it, even when I was afraid. Your presence has been my guide, my comfort, and my strength through every step of this healing journey. You have shown me that it is safe to feel, to cry, to love, to speak, and to be seen. This book was channeled through your light. I simply asked to be a vessel for healing—and you delivered with grace, clarity, and so much love.

To my dear friend Katrina ("Kat")—
Your reading was the spark that lit this fire. When you told me, "I see you writing a book that will help thousands," something shifted. You gave me permission to dream bigger, to step outside my comfort zone, and to believe that my words could make a difference. I was inspired—and terrified—but I'm so grateful I listened.

To Saturn—
Our friendship has been a sacred gift. You've seen me in my darkest places and still loved me with unwavering loyalty. You've pulled me into joy, adventure, and freedom when I needed it most. I'll never forget the call when you finished this book—your tears, your words, "I'm so proud of you... this book changed so much for me." You gave me the confirmation I didn't know I needed. Knowing that this

work moved you—someone who "doesn't do self-help books"—assured me that it would meet people exactly where they are, and that it would truly serve.

To my spiritual sisters—
Thank you for walking this path with me. For the laughter, the tears, the wisdom, the rituals, the deep conversations, and the sacred spaces we've held for one another. Each of you has taught me something, and together, you've become my chosen family. I am endlessly grateful for your presence in my life.

To my clients—
You have been some of my greatest teachers. Your courage, your honesty, and your willingness to do the hard work of healing has inspired me more than words can express. Thank you for allowing me to witness your growth. You have helped shape the tools, stories, and soul of this book.

To the practices—
Meditation, breathwork, movement, and prayer—thank you for being my medicine. You helped me access the truth when words failed, and helped me regulate and rise when I felt like falling.

To everyone who has crossed my path in grace or pain—you've helped me become the woman who could write these words. Thank you.

TABLE OF CONTENTS

Part - I 1
    Chapter 1 3
    Chapter 2 9
    Chapter 3 18
    Chapter 4 25
Part - II 31
    Chapter 5 33
    Chapter 6 40
    Chapter 7 50
    Chapter 8 55
    Chapter 9 60
    Chapter 10 70
    Chapter 11 77
    Chapter 12 82
Part - III 89
    Chapter 13 91
    Chapter 14 107
    Chapter 15 113
From My Heart to Yours 116
About the Author 117

PART - I

Awakening

"And the day came when the risk to remain tight in a bud was more painful than the risk it took to blossom." — Anaïs Nin.

You are standing at the edge of change. You can see the path laid out of healing, yet you are teetering on the edge, wondering if it is worth it.

Wondering if you are strong enough to make it through. Wondering if the flower you will bloom into will ever come to fruition.

It will be my dear friend! You were born to bloom like the lotus flower comes from the depths of the mud, fighting the darkest depths of the water, to burst to the surface with its beautiful bloom. This is your time to bloom!

The healing you seek is yours for the taking if you are willing to take that leap of faith! The first step was picking up this book and now reading the content it contains.

Open your mind, heart, and soul and allow the words that speak to your depths shedding light on what you need to return to yourself. The version of you that existed before all of the things holding you back took their hold on you.

Now is your time!

CHAPTER 1

A Portal to Healing

"Your wound is not your fault, but healing it is your responsibility. That is the greatest act of love you can give yourself."

What if everything that has happened to you—every twist, every heartache, every challenge—was leading you to this very moment?

This moment where you slow down.

This moment is where you reconnect with your inner knowing, your inner healing, and your inner peace.

What if I told you that all of it—the beauty and the pain—has a purpose? That even the hardest seasons of your life carry value?

Not because they were fair or easy but because they hold sacred lessons that can lead you back to wholeness.

Life is a series of experiences, not good, not bad, but experiences. All of them working together for our greater good. We are not going through life, we are growing through life!

When we begin to heal the past and lean into the wisdom hidden in our experiences, life opens. We soften. We grow. And what we discover is that life can be richer, deeper, and more beautiful than we ever imagined.

This book is an offering. A companion for your journey.

It was born from a deep inner calling—a message from Spirit that honestly terrified me at first. But it wouldn't leave me alone. Over time, I realized it wasn't just a nudge—it was a divine assignment.

These pages are filled with wisdom gathered through decades of personal healing, client work, study, and sacred practice. They reflect the tears I've shed, the lessons I've learned, the transformations I've witnessed.

My prayer is that this book finds you exactly when you need it. That it meets you with grace.

That it reminds you: You are not broken. You are becoming.

And that it brings you deep healing, peace, and self-love as you walk your own sacred path.

Hearing Spirits Call

There have been several defining moments in my life where everything shifted—but two stand out as the most profound and life-changing.

I will never forget the first time I heard Spirit's voice—clear as day.

I had been in a long and difficult marriage for twelve years. My husband and I had been together off and on since I was fourteen. Just before he left for a month-long hunting trip, I discovered he had been cheating. I was devastated—but I kept going. For two weeks, I solo-parented our boys. We made it to every football practice, finished homework, got dinners on the table—and, to my surprise, everything ran more smoothly than usual. The house was calm. The boys were getting along. And I was sleeping better than I had in years despite everything going on.

One night, lying in bed, reflecting on that peace, Spirit came through—loud and clear:

"Why are you staying? He isn't loyal. He is mean to you and the kids."

I broke down. That moment shattered the illusions I had been clinging to. I realized I had stayed out of fear—fear of being alone, fear of judgment, fear of failing. I had never lived on my own. I went straight from my parents' house into that marriage. And I was part of a family and church where divorce was deeply discouraged—at least from my perspective. But at that moment, I knew I had to leave.

Taking the First Steps

Years later, I was free of my ex-husband, but emotionally I was still broken. After a series of failed relationships and friendships, I realized something had to change. I was a therapist—I knew I had stored trauma. I had lived through enough to recognize the signs. But I couldn't access the memories, and the few I could remember felt distant like I was describing a client's story—not my own

Releasing Through Movement

Then, one day, I injured my shoulder and couldn't go to the gym, my safe place. A physical therapist suggested yoga. With no studios nearby, I turned to YouTube.

A few days in, I found myself in a Pigeon pose—and suddenly, tears poured from my eyes. I didn't know why. I just knew I needed it. I sat on my mat and cried for thirty minutes. And afterward, I felt lighter than I ever had before.

From that moment on, I was hooked. This pattern continued for months; the more I practiced, the lighter and better I felt!

Taking the First Steps

The healing I experienced didn't come through talking—it came through my body. I didn't have to revisit every traumatic memory. I didn't know why or how, but I knew I was finally releasing what I had been holding. This wasn't something I had learned in grad school, but it changed everything. I dove into research and devoured every book I could find on the mind-body

connection. *Emotional Yoga* by Bija Bennett changed my understanding of how emotions are stored in the body, how they rise when we're ready to release them, and how presence is the key to freedom.

This book is the culmination of all that I've learned—through personal pain, deep healing, spiritual connection, and almost two decades of supporting clients on their own paths. It's not a step-by-step method or a rigid guide.

It's an offering. A sacred path. A light to walk beside you in love. Here's what I want you to know:

- ❖ Healing is not linear.
- ❖ You are not broken.
- ❖ You don't have to "fix" yourself.
- ❖ You only have to come home to yourself.

Throughout this book, I refer to Spirit—you may use whatever name speaks to you: the Divine, the Universe, God, Source. This path honors all beliefs and invites you into a deeper connection—within yourself and the divine.

This is a book for the wounded healer. The overthinker. The one trying to do it all. The seeker. The sensitive soul. The burned-out, the barely hanging on, and the beautiful humans who keep showing up even when they feel like falling apart.

You'll find science here. You'll find spirituality. You'll find stories—mine, my clients' (always with care editing identifiable details), and maybe even your own reflections echoed back to you. This is a companion, not a prescription. A conversation, not a command. Let your heart be your guide.

You'll find tools, affirmations, rituals, and reframes. You'll find permission— to slow down, to grieve, to let go, to rise, to find a deep love for yourself.

Most of all, you'll find the reminder you've been needing: You are light.

Not because you are perfect.

But because you have always carried truth, love, and healing within you. Let this book be a mirror to help you remember.

Take a breath. Settle in. You don't have to have it all figured out.- In fact, sometimes it works out better if we have no idea where we are going.

Because then, we get out of the way and allow Spirit to give us something even better than we can ever imagine.

Your healing journey begins here!

Journal Prompts

1. *Hearing Spirit's Call*

    ❖ When have you felt a quiet nudge, inner voice, or knowing guiding you toward change?

    ❖ If you slowed down and really listened—what is your spirit whispering to you right now?

2. *Taking the First Steps*

    ❖ What fears or beliefs have kept you from stepping fully onto your healing path?

    ❖ What is one small, brave step you can take toward healing today?

3. *Releasing Through Emotion and Movement*

    ❖ When was the last time you allowed yourself to feel without judgment?

    ❖ What practices (like movement, breath, sound, or stillness) help you release stored emotions?

4. *Your Story as a Portal*

- ❖ What painful or transformative experience in your life might be a doorway to deeper healing?

- ❖ How has your past prepared you to hold space for others (or yourself) in new ways?

5. *Awakening Your Light*

    - ❖ What parts of you feel forgotten, dimmed, or hidden?

    - ❖ What does it mean to you to "remember your light"? Describe that version of you in vivid detail.

CHAPTER 2

The Power of Presence - The First Step Toward Healing

"You are only ever one breath away from peace."

--Unknown

Learning to Be Present

This journey is not for the faint of heart. I grappled over where to start and came to the conclusion that we need to begin with supportive practices— tools to help you cope and manage the healing process from the beginning.

We are often unaware of what's going on in our bodies or emotions, especially if we've experienced trauma. Many clients I work with don't remember much of their childhood and are completely out of touch with their bodies.

This chapter is about learning to become more present and aware—of our bodies, thoughts, and emotional patterns—so we can shift from surviving life to responding to it in a way that aligns with our morals, values, and goals.

Anchoring in Awareness

When we're not present, we tend to live caught between regret and grief over the past and anxiety about the future. We stay in survival mode, reacting out of old patterns. We see and experience the world through old filters. Keeping us stuck in survival mode not even realizing that there is something better for us out there.

We cannot change what we are not aware of! The best way I know to change this is through presence. Becoming aware of what is happening in our minds and bodies gives us the power to choose something different.

Presence allows us to catch our thoughts, regulate our breath, recognize body cues, and build the capacity to respond instead of react. It is simple—but not easy. I know many people are looking for quick fixes. I also know some of you are thinking, "Kim, I've tried this. It didn't work."

And to that, I say: How long did you practice?

Our culture is built on instant gratification—fast food, streaming, same-day shipping. But healing doesn't work that way. If you've lived 35 years in survival mode, you won't undo that in a few weeks of therapy and five-minute meditations. Research tells us it takes an average of 66 days to form a new habit. In learning to be more present, we are literally rewiring our brain to change responses and old behavior patterns. This takes time, patience, and extended effort. It has to become a lifestyle, not a thing we do sometimes.

Healing in Layers

In my own journey, I've learned that healing often comes in layers. Our body lets us know when it's ready to release what no longer serves us. An experience may seem healed, only to return in a new form when we're ready to address another layer.

For example, I spent 12 years working in a prison with severely mentally ill inmates. After I left, it took time to reset my nervous system. At first, I had to learn that I didn't need to be on constant alert. That was one layer. Later, I became less reactive to crowds and loud noises. One night, while out with a friend, a woman on a stool laughed really loud, and the stool made a loud bang. I jumped out of my seat, hand instinctively going to where my alarm used to be, ready to shout, "Get down!" We laughed afterward—but the reflex was real. I can proudly say that reflex no longer exists!

Years later, I realized I was still holding onto another trauma layer from that time:

the constant urgency. I always felt like I needed to rush and get ahead. Spirit showed me how that sense of urgency came from years of working in an understaffed, high-stress environment. Even though my life had calmed down, that imprint remained. I became intentional about watching for the signs—thoughts like "I need to hurry," sensations of stress—and I consciously replaced them with a new truth: "I have all the time, resources, and intelligence I need to be successful." Then, I'd take a few deep breaths and bring myself back to peace.

I also realized that although my world had slowed down consistently, I was constantly running late.

Our subconscious craves the chaos we are used to over the peace our conscious mind wants.

Through presence, I realized what I was doing to myself. I would wait until the last minute and make myself late, creating the chaos my subconscious was craving when there was awareness around that I was able to shift this behavior that was causing me so much stress. Now that I wake early, I allow myself time to prepare for my day and space to do all the things I need to do slowly without having to rush. Because I was aware of the sensations in my body, which gave me a clue I was stressed, I was able to begin to shift the behavior.

Living mindfully is a daily practice. It's catching your mind when it wanders and bringing it back over and over—until one day, it happens more naturally. And one day, it gets easier.

Practicing Everyday Mindfulness

If we're not present, we miss opportunities to grow and heal. We react to the world without awareness of our triggers, filters, or how our behavior affects those around us.

The same is true for emotional triggers. We often think they're caused by something external—but they're internal cues that point to what still needs healing. For me, stress shows up as a tight jaw or an eye twitch. I used to ignore those signs. Now I know they're messages from my body, asking me to slow down.

I worked with a client who had a high-stress job managing a huge distribution center. She used to have intense emotional outbursts—panic attacks, crying spells, or explosive anger. We identified a pattern: she was rushing from the moment she woke up, arriving at work with just enough time to clock in, and then reacting to everything at work. She realized this rush created stress, which set the tone for the day. Arriving and staying stressed did not leave space between situations and reactions to them.

We made changes. She simplified his morning routine so she could leave the house earlier. She spent 15–30 minutes doing breathwork and meditation in the car before entering the building. She gave herself time to sit at her desk with a cup of coffee before the day began. These changes shifted everything. She was calmer.

She could handle stress with ease. She said that mindfulness gave her space to breathe, to regulate, and to respond instead of reacting to the chaos of her job.

Without awareness, we cannot shift anything. So what is mindfulness, really?

I define it as being as present as possible, as often as possible. When you notice you're not present, bring yourself back.

That's it. You can practice it anywhere—while cooking, walking, folding laundry, or watering your garden. Meditation helps, but mindfulness is a way of living, not just the minutes you sit quietly.

Start small. Choose one task to do mindfully. Sit for three minutes, focusing on your breath. Set reminders on your phone that say, "Where is your mind right now?" When it goes off, take three grounding breaths, place your feet on the floor, and return to yourself.

Mindfulness doesn't require incense or a meditation cushion. It requires willingness. And it takes practice.

Debunking Mindfulness Myths Mindfulness means clearing your mind.

Not true. The goal is awareness, not emptiness. Everyone has thoughts. The gift of mindfulness is learning; you can choose to observe the thoughts without engaging with them.

1. **Mindfulness is only meditation.**

Meditation is one path, but you can practice mindfulness while walking, eating, or folding laundry.

2. **It's a quick fix.**

It takes time, consistency, and compassion.

3. **It's just a relaxation technique.**

It can be relaxing, but its purpose is awareness and acceptance—not constant bliss.

4. **It's only for spiritual people.**

Mindfulness is evidence-based and used in therapy, schools, hospitals, and workplaces.

5. **You need hours to practice.**

A few minutes, a few times a day, makes a difference.

6. **It's about always feeling good.**

It's about being with whatever it is—grief, joy, fear, pain—and letting it move through you.

7. **It's about controlling emotions.**

It's not about suppression. It's about learning to ***respond*** rather than ***react***. Observer rather than engage. Be rather than do.

You're not here to be perfect. You're here to be present. To return to yourself. To meet your life with open eyes, a grounded body, and a heart willing to grow.

In my humble opinion, presence is the key to everything. Nothing can change unless we're aware it's happening. Is it hard to stay present? Yes. Is it difficult to sit in meditation and bring your attention back 500,000 times a minute? Yes. Can it be frustrating beyond measure? Yes.

Is it worth it? Absolutely.

If you want peace, joy, self-love, and the abundantly blessed life you deserve, it is 100% necessary.

But How?

Here is a great beginner practice that I teach all of my clients:

- ❖ Begin with a short mindful meditation practice daily, 3-5 minutes of focussing on your breath. Breathe in calm, breathe out letting go of stress. Those words can be replaced with whatever you are calling in and whatever you desire to release.

- ❖ For the next 3-5 minutes set an intention to be present throughout your day. Practice presence by observing your thoughts. If you catch your mind in the past or the future gently with compassion bring yourself

❖ back to the present moment.

❖ End with another 3-5 minutes focusing on the breath or picking some form of breath work to practice to finish off.

Try bringing mindfulness into everyday activities. Pick activities in your day-to-day life and intentionally slow down and do them mindfully.

A good place to start is sitting down to eat a meal. Take in the aroma of goodness you are about to eat. As you place it in your mouth, fully taste and savor it. Take time to chew it and be present while you eat it. Notice how it makes you feel. Do you feel more nourished and content when you eat mindfully?

You might also choose to practice mindful conversations with loved ones. Really listening to what they are saying without thinking about your response to them or your similar stories. Be present and really listen to what they are saying, taking in the energy they project around what is being said. Doing your best to really hear and understand them.

Take mindful walks, taking in the surroundings, turning off the music or audiobook! Try to find something new on your daily commute to observe.

There are opportunities everywhere for us to practice being present. Start small, pick one or two things and build from there.

Be kind to yourself. This takes time to learn! Some days will be easier than others, but allow yourself to show up for what is, no matter how it seems to be that day. Celebrate the wins and love yourself through the harder days.

Affirmations

❖ I am here. I am now. I am safe.

❖ Each breath brings me back to myself.

❖ I choose presence over perfection.

- ❖ My awareness is my power.
- ❖ I meet this moment with compassion.
- ❖ I am grounded, centered, and calm.
- ❖ I release the past and soften into the now.
- ❖ I allow myself to pause and just be.
- ❖ The more present I become, the more peace I feel.
- ❖ I trust that healing happens one breath at a time.

Journal Prompts

1. When do I feel most present and connected to myself?
2. What helps me access that state?
3. In what ways do I tend to leave the present moment (e.g., overthinking, worrying, distraction)?
4. What physical or emotional signs tell me that I'm disconnected from the here and now?
5. What might change in my life if I practiced mindful awareness more consistently?
6. How do I currently respond to discomfort or emotional triggers—and how could presence shift that?
7. What does "being present" mean to me in this season of life?
8. What daily activities could I turn into mindful rituals, even for just a few minutes a day?
9. What old story or fear tells me I need to stay busy, distracted, or on alert? Am I ready to release that belief?

10. How do I speak to myself when I notice I've drifted away from my presence? Could I offer myself more compassion?

11. What would it feel like to approach my healing journey one breath at a time?

CHAPTER 3

The Mind is a Trickster — A New Relationship with Thoughts

"Why do you stay in prison when the door is so wide open?"

— Rumi

The mind is incredibly powerful. It can be the greatest tool for healing—or the biggest source of suffering.

In my practice over the past 5 years, I have treated predominantly people suffering with Obsessive Compulsive Disorder. This is a disorder commonly misunderstood, misdiagnosed, and mistreated. To have OCD, you must have an unwanted obsessional thought, which brings severe anxiety.

These thoughts can include anything. I have treated people who were afraid they would harm themselves or someone else. I have worked with people who were afraid they were child molesters even though they knew they would never do such a thing. I have people who feared they were straight/gay when they knew they were not and people who questioned many bizarre and unusual things about their life! The obsessions love to attack the things we most value in our life which is why it makes it so hard to manage.

There must also be a compulsion that is an attempt to decrease the anxiety around the obsession. The commonly known ones are physical compulsions like checking doors, locks and stoves. The commonly missed compulsions are mental rumination (trying to figure it all out), asking for reassurance from others, researching every possible solution to the fear, and avoiding the triggers to the fear. But really, compulsions can be anything you are doing to "urgently make the anxiety go away."

The method I teach you in this chapter will help you free you from the prison of your mind. Not by challenging fears or anxious thoughts but by sitting with them and allowing them to exist. Allowing anxiety to come and to go without engaging in the compulsions, trying to force it to go away.

Recognize Unhelpful Thinking Patterns

One of the biggest game changers in my healing was learning that just because I think something doesn't make it true.

Thoughts like:

- ❖ "They hate me."
- ❖ "I'm going to fail."
- ❖ "I'm not good enough."
- ❖ "I can't handle this."
- ❖ "I'm stupid."

...are not facts. They are just thoughts. But when we believe them, they shape our emotional experience, our behavior, and ultimately our lives.

It's important to begin observing these thoughts without attaching to them. Notice them without judgment. Let them come and go like clouds passing through the sky.

Sitting with Fear

Sometimes, though, those thoughts can feel incredibly sticky—especially when they show up as fear.

A common response to fear-based thoughts is to try to push them away, challenge them, or "think positively." But for those with intense anxiety—especially social anxiety or obsessive-compulsive patterns—this often backfires. Trying to convince yourself that the fear isn't true only reinforces the fear's power.

We can change what we sit with, not what we run from!

Sometimes, our mind/anxiety/fear can be like the big bad bully on the playground. The more the bully picks on us, and we run from the bully or cower to it, the more afraid we get and the more the bully picks on us!

When we stand up to the bully on the playground what happens? We might have a fight on our hands but the bully will generally back down and pick on an easier target.

In this scenario, the bully is our social anxiety, picking on everything we do. The bully is our fear of calling a friend we have not talked to in a while for fear of what they might think. The anxiety we have around doing anything is because we have some obsessional thought that it won't work or it will cause us harm.

The more we run from the feared thing or anxiety-provoking thought, the more we reinforce the connection between the feared thing and our need to avoid it.

Instead, I teach clients a different approach—one rooted in mindfulness and exposure therapy.

If a thought arises, like "They probably think I'm weird," instead of arguing with it, what if we welcomed it?

What if we said:

- ❖ "Yes, they might think I'm weird."

- ❖ "They might not like me."

❖ "They may even think I'm too much or not enough."

And then… we let that be okay. We allow our fear, anxiety, and all the emotions to come up around it. Leaning into the feared thoughts over and over until the fear passes.

I know this sounds counterintuitive, but in my private practice, where I specialize in treating anxiety disorders, including OCD, I've seen how powerful this approach can be. Many of my clients have been stuck in the prison of their own thoughts their entire life. Traditionally, if someone has a fear of snakes, we slowly expose them to a snake so the brain learns it can be around the snake—it may never love the snake, but it also doesn't need to run from the room.

The same is true for the thoughts we fear. If we sit with the feared thoughts long enough, the brain eventually gets bored. The thoughts lose their power.

This is the practice of sitting with discomfort instead of trying to make it go away. Allowing the anxiety to rise—and trusting that it will also fall. This teaches the brain: I can handle this. I don't have to fight it. I don't have to believe it. I can just feel it and let it pass.

This is where mindfulness and healing intersect in a powerful way. Mindfulness teaches us to observe. To witness. To allow. Not to fix or control—but to be with.

When we stop resisting our fear, we begin to disarm it.

That's not to say there's anything wrong with challenging thoughts or using affirmations. I absolutely believe in those tools and use them often. But if those tools don't work for you—or if you've tried them and felt worse—it's okay. There's another path.

In those moments, try saying:

"This thought is here. I'm willing to feel what it brings up. I don't need to push it away. I'm safe to feel it."

And if that feels like too much, I want you to know you don't have to do this alone. These practices can be intense, and for some people—especially those with trauma or OCD—it's wise to work with a therapist trained in Exposure Response Prevention (ERP) and mindfulness-based approaches.

Your healing journey should never feel like punishment. You deserve support, safety, and kindness as you learn to be with your inner world.

Observing Without Engaging

And one last thing I want you to remember:

The mind is a trickster. But it's not your enemy. It's trying to keep you safe. It's repeating the stories it thinks will protect you. Your subconscious drives a lot of your emotions and behaviors. It assumes that the past is safer because you've already experienced it. As you begin to step into the unknown, your subconscious becomes afraid—creating anxiety to try to keep you in familiar territory.

Our job isn't to destroy the mind—it's to teach it that we're safe now. That we're capable. That we're growing.

So the next time a fear-based thought shows up, pause. Breathe. Invite it in if you can. Or gently place it to the side. Trust that it's okay to feel—and it's also okay not to engage.

Your thoughts are not your reality. They're simply echoes of the past or fears about the future, trying to trick you into avoiding the unknown to stay safe.

But you are safe. You are capable. You are growing.

Embodiment Practice: Becoming the Watcher

As you close this chapter, take a few moments to sit quietly and become aware of your thoughts.

Notice what arises without needing to change it. Imagine each thought as a leaf floating down a stream. Some drift gently, others tumble and swirl—but none of them stay forever.

Place one hand on your heart and the other on your belly. Breathe deeply. Repeat silently:

"I am not my thoughts. I am the one who watches."

Let yourself feel the freedom in that truth. You are the observer. You are the space between the thoughts. You are the calm center beneath the chaos.

Affirmations

Use these to reinforce a new, empowering relationship with your mind.

- ❖ I am not my thoughts. I am the one who watches.
- ❖ Just because I think it doesn't make it true.
- ❖ I observe my mind with compassion and curiosity.
- ❖ My thoughts do not control me—I choose what to believe.
- ❖ I am safe to feel discomfort and let it pass.
- ❖ My truth is stronger than my fear.
- ❖ I trust my ability to meet my thoughts with peace and presence.
- ❖ Each moment is a chance to choose a more loving belief.

Journal Prompts

Invite deeper self-inquiry and reflection on thought patterns and mental healing.

1. What recurring thought patterns keep me stuck in fear, self-doubt, or limitation?

2. How does my body respond when I'm caught in anxious or critical thoughts?

3. What does it feel like when I observe my thoughts instead of reacting to them?

4. What is one anxiety or fear-provoking thought I am willing to experiment and sit with, allowing the anxiety to rise and fall on its own so I can regain my power over it?

CHAPTER 4

The Healing Power of Gratitude — Anchoring Joy in the Present

"Acknowledging the good that you already have in your life is the foundation for all abundance."

— Eckhart Tolle

Choosing a Grateful Lens

Gratitude is one of the simplest yet most powerful healing tools we have. It shifts our perspective from what's missing to what's already here. It brings us into the present moment, softens fear, and rewires the brain toward peace, joy, and abundance.

This isn't about pretending everything is okay when it's not. Gratitude doesn't ask us to deny pain—it invites us to hold both. It allows us to honor what is hard while still noticing what is good, what is beautiful, and what is quietly holding us together.

You don't need grand gestures. Gratitude begins with small moments: the warmth of a mug in your hands, the sound of birds outside your window, the rhythm of your breath. These seemingly simple moments are anchors. They remind us that even when life feels uncertain, something steady and sacred remains.

One of the stories I will never forget is the story of a lifer who changed my understanding of gratitude. I had received a new patient from another prison. In reading his story, I realized that at this other institution, he had a good job; he had started a Lifer's Group, which was successful, and was doing well there. Having received many inmates from this institution in the past, knowing it was set in a beautiful place with a lot more programming opportunities, most inmates were angry and depressed about arriving at our not-so-beautiful area. Especially since he left his job, friends, and the successful program he had started there. I called him into my office, ready to process his grief. To my utter shock, the session went very differently than I expected! He was overjoyed to be there! With sheer surprise in my voice, I asked why he was so happy to be here. He explained at his previous institution they could not see past the walls. The window to his dorm faced the back side of the institution where the train tracks laid. Trains passed by multiple times throughout the day.

He explained that this reminded him that there was a life out there, and one day, he might be able to be out there again living it!

I had worked with many other inmates who hated this. Their perception was that this was a reminder of a life they were currently not allowed to live.

They interpreted it as a negative thing.

This inmate was so focussed on his gratitude for being able to see something better he had not even noticed what he had left behind at the previous institution. He had a positive filter that was looking for the best in things. Because he had this positive filter, he remained positive even through a tough transition that would have challenged most people.

Most of us don't realize how often our thoughts are running on autopilot, shaped by years of conditioning, trauma, and habit. These patterns form a lens through which we see the world, and we often mistake those thoughts for truth.

If we can become aware of this pattern, and recognize our filters, we can shift our beliefs and experiences in our life.

Gratitude and the Nervous System

From a mental health and somatic perspective, gratitude activates the parasympathetic nervous system—the "rest and digest" state. When we pause and intentionally focus on what we appreciate, we send a signal to the brain: "It's safe to soften."

This allows our bodies to regulate more easily, our minds to slow down, and our emotions to move through us instead of taking over. Gratitude creates space in the body for healing and peace.

A Personal Story of Perspective

There have been many seasons in my life where I've felt overwhelmed— when things seemed hard, sticky, or completely impossible. But it's in those times I've learned that returning to gratitude helps shift my perspective.

When I'm feeling weighed down, it can be hard to find things I'm grateful for. In those moments, I return to nature.

I go outside and sit on my rock—the place where I often meditate, cry, ground, and commune with Spirit in my yard. It brings me joy to watch my chickens peck around, to see birds and butterflies fluttering through the yard without a care in the world. It brings me peace to watch the sunlight sparkle through the trees. These moments help me shift, even when life feels like it's beyond repair. I can always find gratitude in the small things.

I've seen this same shift happen with clients. I remember a woman I worked with who was going through a long, painful divorce. Every session was heavy with grief and anger. One day, I gently asked her, "Can you name one thing you're grateful for today?" She paused for a long time, then said, "I guess... my dog. She always curls up next to me when I cry."

That became her anchor. Week after week, she added more: her morning coffee, the scent of rain, the support of a friend. Her circumstances didn't magically change—but her energy did. She began to find strength in small joys, and those small joys created the capacity for healing.

Gratitude became the doorway back to presence.

Gratitude and High Vibration Living

In his book *Letting Go*, Dr. David R. Hawkins shares the concept of the hierarchy of human emotions and their corresponding vibrational frequencies. On this scale, emotions like shame, guilt, and fear vibrate at lower levels—often leaving us feeling stuck, heavy, or disconnected. But as we begin to move into higher vibrational states like gratitude, acceptance, love, and peace, our entire energy field begins to shift.

Gratitude is one of the highest vibrational emotions, sitting just below love and peace. When we cultivate gratitude consistently, we naturally elevate our emotional frequency. We start to feel lighter, more hopeful, and more connected to our inner truth and to the world around us. The more we choose gratitude, the more resilient we become to the stressors of life.

This doesn't mean we ignore hard things. It means we train ourselves to hold discomfort while also staying anchored in something higher. When we live in a high-vibrational state—through gratitude, joy, love, and compassion— we're less likely to be brought down by negativity or outside chaos. Our nervous system becomes more regulated, our minds more focused, and our hearts more open.

Gratitude is more than a tool. It's a frequency. And the more we live there, the more we invite healing, alignment, and deep inner peace.

Gratitude as a Daily Practice

You don't need hours or elaborate rituals. You just need presence. Try this:

- ❖ Start or end your day by writing down three things you're grateful for.

- ❖ When something difficult happens, ask: "Is there still something here I can appreciate?"

- ❖ Speak your gratitude out loud—especially to the people you love.

- ❖ Close your eyes and feel gratitude in your body. Let it expand gently.

Affirmations for Gratitude & High-Vibration Living

- ❖ I choose to see the beauty in this moment.
- ❖ Even in the midst of a challenge, I can find something to be grateful for.
- ❖ Gratitude connects me to peace, joy, and presence.
- ❖ I honor both the light and the lessons in my life.
- ❖ I welcome more of what nourishes me and releases what drains me.
- ❖ My energy rises when I anchor into appreciation.
- ❖ Gratitude is my daily practice and sacred medicine.
- ❖ I am worthy of receiving the abundance life offers me.
- ❖ Each breath is a gift. Each moment is a blessing.

Gratitude Doesn't Need to Be Earned

You don't have to wait until everything is perfect to feel grateful. In fact, it's the act of finding gratitude in the imperfect that teaches us how resilient and whole we truly are. Gratitude isn't a reward. It's a practice. And when practiced consistently, it becomes a powerful medicine.

Let it be simple. Let it be messy. Let it be enough.

Let gratitude remind you of the joy that still exists—right here, right now.

Journal Prompts

1. What are three small things I'm grateful for today—no matter how simple?
2. When I pause to notice the beauty around me, what do I see?
3. What has a difficult experience in my life taught me that I now appreciate?
4. How do I feel in my body and spirit when I focus on gratitude?
5. Who or what brings light into my life, and how can I express appreciation for them?
6. How has gratitude helped me shift my perspective or regulate my nervous system?
7. What would it look like to make gratitude a daily ritual in my life?
8. How can I return to gratitude when I feel overwhelmed or disconnected?

PART - II

Healing & Integration

"One does not become enlightened by imagining figures of light, but by making the darkness conscious." - Carl Jung.

I have seen several people in my lifetime of work who know all the right things to do but somehow remain the same. If I'm honest with myself, there have been times where I have seen the way and chose a different path in life.

The lasting change is not in knowing the right things but in doing the work. Even when it is hard, feels hopeless, or feels overwhelming, you show up for yourself time and time again until the work and the way become second nature. Until we follow the path we know is right for our soul!

This section is about following the path less traveled. Diving deep into your shadows, accepting, healing, and growing through all of it. It inspires us to rewire automatic thinking patterns that shape our behaviors. We are called to sit with and work through the stored and current emotions that get in the way of our peace, love, and joy!

If you accept the journey into the darkest parts of yourself and do the hard work of rewiring and letting go, there is joy, peace, and self-love beyond your understanding on the other side.

See you on the other side, my dear friend!

CHAPTER 5

Embracing the Shadow — When Spirit Sends Triggers to Guide Us

"The wound is the place where the Light enters you."

— *Rumi*

I have read and seen many explanations of the "Shadow" and found it confusing and hard to understand at times what "Shadow Work" is. In this chapter I will not only attempt to explain what the Shadow is but also how to accept it and integrate it as part of you. It truly is a beautiful thing to love and accept all the parts of us without shame, guilt, or an explanation! No one is perfect, and if the world was filled with a bunch of perfect people, it would be a very boring place to live!

In this chapter, we will integrate the hidden and avoided parts of us. Shedding light and love on them, fully accepting all of the parts of ourselves. There is freedom in coming out of the darkness, being brave enough to show our shadows to ourselves allowing healing and integration.

Shadows Explained

Every one of us has a shadow—a part of ourselves we've rejected, ignored, or denied. The shadow is made up of everything we've pushed away because it didn't feel safe, acceptable, or lovable. It's the unconscious part of our psyche that holds our pain, our fears, and even our power. This is the side of us shaped by childhood wounds, generational trauma, cultural expectations, and survival patterns. It's not inherently bad—it's simply unintegrated. The shadow is created when we disconnect from parts of ourselves in order to be accepted, avoid rejection, or stay emotionally and physically safe. And yet, those very parts often hold our creativity, passion, emotional depth, and truth.

It's the side of us we try to hide—the part we think is too much, too angry, too sensitive, too needy, too emotional, too scared, too bad, too dirty.

Often, our shadow was born out of survival. We buried parts of ourselves because, at one point, it was not safe to express them. Our shadows shape our behavior and often relate to the areas of our lives where we feel guilt, shame, disgust, or embarrassment. It's the part of us that turns to unhealthy coping strategies—things we might call "sinful pleasures"—to numb the pain or feel connected to something. It's also the part that may draw us into toxic relationships because, deep down, we believe we don't deserve better. If we look closely at our patterns, reactions, and triggers, we will always find clues to our shadows.

Naming the Shadow

Shadow work is the brave act of turning toward these parts of ourselves with curiosity and compassion rather than shame. And often, Spirit uses our external life to reveal what still lives in our internal world.

Understanding Emotional Triggers

Triggers, for example, are not here to torment us—they're here to illuminate what's unhealed.

That co-worker who dismisses your ideas? Maybe she's revealing your fear of not being good enough. That moment of rage when someone interrupts you? Maybe it's your inner child screaming to be heard. That panic you feel when your partner withdraws? Maybe it's a mirror of abandonment wounds from long ago.

I once worked with a man who, by all external measures, was highly successful. He was a top executive in his company, owned multiple properties, drove luxury cars, and was admired by his peers. But internally, he was exhausted, anxious, and deeply disconnected. He came to therapy because he was experiencing panic attacks and couldn't sleep through the night. He described feeling like he was constantly "performing" and afraid the mask might slip.

At first, he couldn't understand why he felt so hollow. He had everything he thought he was supposed to want—but none of it brought peace. As we dug deeper, we discovered a powerful shadow belief:

"I am only valuable if I achieve. If I stop performing, I will be rejected or forgotten."

His childhood had been marked by conditional love. Praise came only with accomplishment—good grades, trophies, stoicism. Emotional vulnerability was seen as a weakness. Somewhere along the way, he internalized the belief that his worth was tied to his output. Rest felt lazy. Asking for help felt shameful. Slowing down felt dangerous.

This shadow of unworthiness wore the mask of perfectionism and productivity. And it was slowly destroying him.

In our work together, he began to notice how deeply this belief was embedded—not just in his work life but in his relationships and his self-talk. He struggled to be emotionally present with his partner, to connect with his children, or even to relax alone. Every moment of stillness triggered an inner voice that screamed, *"You're falling behind."*

We began to gently challenge that voice through mindfulness, somatic work, and inner child healing. He learned to be with the discomfort instead of reacting to it. He practiced resting without guilt, celebrating himself without accomplishment, and connecting with others without proving his worth. He even started taking slow walks in the woods before work—a ritual that felt rebellious at first but soon became sacred.

Over time, he discovered that beneath all the striving was a scared little boy who just wanted to be loved for who he was—not for what he did.

And that's where the healing happened. When he made space for that boy when he held that part of himself with compassion instead of judgment, something shifted. He started living with more ease. He began showing up with more vulnerability in his relationships. He stopped chasing his worth and began embodying it.

His story is a reminder that the shadow isn't always loud or dramatic. Sometimes, it hides in ambition, in over-functioning, in perfectionism. But no matter how it shows up, it holds the same sacred purpose: to guide us back to the truth of who we are. Whole. Worthy. Enough—without doing a thing.

We often think of our triggers or our hard times as horrible and painful. But they're actually sacred invitations.

When we feel triggered, it's easy to blame the situation or the other person. But when we slow down and turn inward, we can find a deeper truth—a message from within that's ready to be seen, held, and healed.

Re-parenting the Wounded Self

When I first began writing this book, I was terrified. I've always been a high achiever, but I've also preferred to stay under the radar. Writing this meant being seen, heard, and vulnerable. It meant telling my story—and that was absolutely terrifying.

I avoided it for months. I procrastinated. I doubted. I got frustrated with myself for not starting sooner.

But when I paused and sat with fear, I realized it wasn't just resistance. It was a part of me—my inner child—who had been told she was too much, too opinionated, too loud. She didn't want to be seen. She wanted to be safe.

Instead of pushing that fear away, I acknowledged her. I said, *"I see you. I understand why you're afraid. But we can do this. We're safe now."*

That shift allowed me to move forward. Not because the fear was gone but because I made space for it—and for her.

When we bring love to the places we once abandoned, we create wholeness.

Shadowwork is not about fixing what's broken. It's about welcoming what's been exiled. It's about realizing that your anger, grief, shame, fear, jealousy— none of them make you bad or unworthy. They make you human.

And the more we allow these parts of us to have a voice, the less they control us from the shadows.

If you're feeling resistant, judgmental, or overwhelmed as you read this— that's okay. That's part of the shadow, too. Bring your awareness to it. Let it be here. Invite it in with love.

I had a client who continuously attracted abusive or neglectful relationships. Each man may have looked different on the surface, but in time, they would become emotionally harmful or suddenly disappear. This pattern left her heartbroken and confused. She was beautiful, intelligent, funny, successful—by all measures, an amazing catch.

As we explored her history, we traced her patterns back to childhood. Her mother was emotionally abusive, often telling her she was hated stupid, and calling her names no child should ever hear. Her father, disconnected and frustrated by the toxic home environment, avoided the household by staying away at work. She never felt loved, safe, or emotionally supported.

These early wounds shaped her belief that she was unlovable. She felt surprised anytime someone liked her. As an adult, she subconsciously sought out men who felt familiar—those who were abusive like her mom or distant like her dad. It was the "love" her inner child knew how to navigate. And the more she tried to prove her worth through kindness and giving, the more these men would leave— confirming her shadow belief that she wasn't enough.

Through deep shadow work, we brought these patterns to light. We worked on re-parenting her inner child and reinforcing new beliefs: *"I am lovable," "I am worthy of love,"* and *"I don't have to earn affection."* Over time, her energy shifted. She entered a new relationship with a kind, emotionally available man—and although it felt uncomfortable at first, she stayed with the process. That relationship changed not only how she saw men but how she saw herself.

Transforming Avoidance Into Wisdom

There is deep medicine in what we avoid. Spirit brings it forward not to punish us but to set us free.

Avoidance often happens around our most obvious wounds. "Trigger warning" has become a common term—and while I fully support people's need to protect themselves from harm, I also believe healing asks us to eventually lean in. We miss opportunities for healing when we run from our triggers.

My ex-husband had a horrendous childhood, which he wore like a badge of honor. When he behaved badly, he blamed his upbringing. "At least I'm not as bad as my dad," he'd say. And while that may have been true, I always came back to the same truth: yes, and you are still responsible for healing. You are not your trauma. You are here to heal your trauma—and in doing so, you help heal the generations that came before and those that will come after.

Choosing to blame or avoid responsibility keeps us stuck. But choosing to meet ourselves honestly—that's where freedom lives.

We heal not by avoiding our triggers but by understanding them. By sitting with discomfort. By listening. By softening. By loving ourselves through all of it!

And little by little, we become whole.

And your healing is unfolding, one thought at a time.

Affirmations

Repeat these aloud or silently as you sit in stillness:

- ❖ I am safe to meet all parts of myself with compassion.
- ❖ My shadows are not shameful—they are sacred teachers.
- ❖ I honor the wisdom within my triggers.
- ❖ I no longer run from my discomfort; I listen to its message.
- ❖ Every part of me is worthy of love and healing.
- ❖ As I embrace my shadows, I become whole.

Journal Prompts

1. What part of myself have I been afraid to look at—and why?
2. Describe a recent trigger. What emotion or memory did it awaken in you?
3. How might that trigger be trying to show you where healing is needed?
4. What part of your inner child is asking to be seen and loved?
5. What do you need to feel safe as you explore your shadow?
6. What would it feel like to bring love to a part of yourself you've rejected?

CHAPTER 6

Change Your Mind, Change Your Life — Rewriting the Stories That Keep You Stuck

"Until you make the unconscious conscious, it will direct your life, and you will call it fate."

— Carl Jung

After shining light on our shadows, it becomes essential to examine the thoughts that feed them. Our beliefs and filters are shaped by childhood experiences which create the emotional terrain we walk every day.

Sometimes, the way we think becomes the very thing that keeps us from healing. Before we can feel, process, or surrender, we need to become aware of how our mind filters the world—and whether those filters are helping or harming us.

This chapter is about learning to work with your thoughts rather than against them. It's about identifying the stories you're telling yourself, questioning whether they're true, and creating space for new beliefs that support your healing and growth.

We've all been shaped by our environment in some way. As Don Miguel Ruiz writes, we are born as perfect, innocent children—and then life happens. We are shaped by the lies people tell us, by the hurts we experience, and by the beliefs we adopt in response. Some experiences build trust and connection; others create wounds that teach us to build walls or reach outside ourselves for safety or validation.

One might assume that harmful thinking patterns only come from obvious negativity—harsh words, criticism, or painful experiences. But that's not always the case. Sometimes, the beliefs that cause us the most suffering come from words that were intended to uplift us.

I've worked with countless clients who, on the surface, seemed to have been encouraged and praised. One client remembered being told, "You're so amazing—you'll be president one day!" Another was often reminded, "Be a good girl while Daddy is gone so I can be proud of you." These statements were offered with love and spoken with the best of intentions. But over time, they planted seeds of pressure and conditional worth.

For these clients, the underlying message they internalized wasn't simply encouragement—it was expectation. They came to believe they had to be the best at everything to earn love and approval. They pushed themselves to overachieve, constantly striving for validation from others, never feeling quite "enough" just as they were.

This reflects something Don Miguel Ruiz teaches in The Four Agreements: as children, we are domesticated through praise and punishment. We make unconscious "agreements" with ourselves based on how others respond to us. Even loving words can create limiting agreements when they tie our worth to performance or goodness. Without realizing it, we live out these silent contracts for decades—believing we must achieve to be loved or behave perfectly to be accepted.

The reality is, love should not be conditional. Your worth is not tied to how much you accomplish or how "good" you are compared to others. True healing invites us to recognize the difference between genuine encouragement and unconscious expectation—and to rewrite the inner agreements that no longer serve our freedom or joy.

Understanding our beliefs and automatic reactions allows us to shift them— to find balance in how we love, protect, and soften when it's safe to do so.

When I worked at the prison and facilitated groups, I used a simple chair exercise. I'd place a chair in the center of the room and ask the group to describe what they saw. Each person viewed the chair from a different angle, and none of them were wrong—they were simply describing it from their own perspective.

This is how life works. When we become aware of how we're interpreting experiences and learn to recognize our automatic thoughts, we create the space to shift them. That's what this chapter offers—a path to uncover, understand, and gently reframe your thinking patterns so they work for you, not against you.

Understanding the Mindset-Emotion-Behavior Loop

At the heart of Cognitive Behavioral Therapy (CBT) is a simple but powerful truth: our thoughts affect how we feel, which affects how we behave. When we shift our thinking, we shift our experience of the world.

Uncovering Limiting Beliefs

I worked in the Mental Health Crisis Bed at the prison for a few years alongside a brilliant psychologist. I was often the only staff member who overlapped with the weekend crew and was responsible for briefing the regular team on Tuesdays.

During a particularly busy week, I kept referring to myself as "stupid" after making small mistakes. Finally, the psychologist—tall, soft-spoken, and deeply insightful—stood over my desk and said, "Kim, you have to stop saying that. You're one of the smartest people I know."

At first, I was annoyed. But during my commute home that night, his words hit me hard. I started crying, realizing he was right. The next morning, I journaled about how often I called myself stupid. I realized it wasn't just a joke—it was a subconscious belief rooted in my upbringing, where joking at others' expense was common, and I'd often been called stupid for making mistakes.

I decided to change that narrative. Every time the thought came up, I challenged it with the truth: I excelled in school, I was respected in my field, and I had always been capable. Within a few months, I had completely rewired that belief—and I no longer thought of myself that way.

Digging Deeper Into Your Own Stories

Most of us carry automatic thoughts that quietly run in the background of our daily lives. They often show up without us even noticing—like a mental reflex. For me, it was the way I used to constantly call myself "stupid" without even thinking about it. These thought patterns can take many forms:

I'm lazy.

I can't do anything right. I'm not good enough.

I'm too much—or not enough.

These inner stories are often so familiar that we don't even question them. But they deeply impact how we feel, how we move through the world, and how much love we allow ourselves to receive.

Pause for a moment and ask yourself:

- ❖ What are some stories I tell myself?
- ❖ When things get hard, what are the automatic thoughts that pop up?
- ❖ How do those thoughts make me feel?
- ❖ How would I rather feel?

If your automatic thoughts leave you feeling small, heavy, or discouraged, it's time to challenge them.

Start by paying attention to your everyday thinking. Notice which thoughts seem to have the biggest impact on your mood and sense of self. Pick just one or two of those recurring thoughts to focus on. Then, choose an affirmation that directly challenges those old beliefs.

Every time the old thought surfaces, gently but firmly replace it with your new affirmation. Repeat it even if it feels awkward at first. Over time, you'll notice something powerful: either the old thought will fade, or the new truth will begin to feel more natural and real.

Once you've shifted one pattern, move on to another one or two. This process may feel slow at first, but each small step creates real, lasting change. Before you know it, you'll find yourself thinking in ways that support you, nurture you, and affirm your worth.

You have the power to rewrite your inner dialogue.

You have the power to turn "stinking thinking" into thoughts that honor your light and show yourself the love you've always deserved.

Cognitive Distortions: The Brain's Default Filters

Our brains are wired to protect us—not always to see clearly. Especially when we're stressed, or in survival mode, we fall into predictable traps called cognitive distortions. These patterns can also stem from childhood messages, trauma, or long-term conditioning.

Here are some common distortions:

❖ **All-or-Nothing Thinking:**

"If I'm not perfect, I've failed." Things are either good or bad—no in-between.

❖ **Catastrophizing:**

"This is the worst thing ever. I'll never recover." We exaggerate and spiral into worst-case scenarios.

❖ **All-or-Nothing Thinking:**

Also known as "black and white thinking," it is the inability to see shades of gray.

> ➢ I'm either perfect or all bad
>
> ➢ It is right or it is wrong

- **Mind Reading.**
    - The assumption that you know what someone is thinking. I know they did that to hurt me. Even though there is no evidence to support that.

- **Should Statements**
    - I should have made more progress with my healing journey by now
    - Meditation should be easy for me by now
    - They should know better or be better

- **Control fallacies.**
    - Feeling you have control over other's behavior, or you have no control over anything
    - If my parents would not have done x then I would be able to keep a job. -feeling you have no control over your life and blaming others for your own behaviors
    - If I would have been a better parent/friend, then they would have stopped using drugs. - feeling you can control other people's behavior and choices

- **Catastrophizing**
    - One small thing happens, but our mind automatically decides that the worst possible outcome will happen and the world is ending

- **Mental Filtering**

> A list of positive things can be given to you with one small bit of constructive criticism and you only hear the one negative thing. You are not able to heal all the good things just said.

❖ **Overgeneralization**

> Drawing broad, negative conclusions about something based on a single experience.

> Deciding you will never be able to learn to meditate because you tried it once, and it was too hard to sit still

❖ **Emotional Reasoning**

> Assuming your feelings are a reflection of reality

> I feel guilty, therefore, I must have done something wrong

These distortions are normal—but they don't have to run the show. When we bring awareness to them, we begin to loosen their grip.

Questioning Your Filters

We view life through lenses shaped by our past—our upbringing, culture, trauma, and relationships. If you relate to several of the distortions above, know that you're not alone. But don't try to tackle them all at once. Start with one or two. When those feel more manageable, move on to others.

Ask Yourself:

❖ "What filters am I using right now?"

❖ "Is this filter true, helpful, and based on facts?"

- ❖ "What else could be true?"
- ❖ "Can I look at this from a new perspective?"

Reframing with Compassion

This isn't about slapping on toxic positivity. It's about gently guiding your mind toward thoughts that support your healing. If your inner critic whispers, "I'm failing," respond with, "I'm doing the best I can with what I have today—and that is more than enough."

If you know you are prone to catastrophize things when you notice you are having a big reaction to something, take some steps back, ask yourself the above questions and shift your filter to something more helpful.

You can also use affirmations to interrupt distorted thinking. When I caught myself saying, "I'm stupid," I'd respond, "Not true. I'm smart. I'm educated. I've earned respect in my work." Over time, these small acts of truth-telling changed my inner landscape.

Standing Up to the Inner Bully

So many of my clients speak to themselves in ways they'd never speak to a loved one. They hold impossible standards and brush off compliments.

Their Inner Bully Runs the Show

If we want to live in peace, we must challenge that bully. We have to start replacing those critical inner voices with love. We must become aware of our filters and challenge them!

I often ask: *"Would you say that to your child? To your best friend?"*

You deserve your own compassion. Be your own cheerleader. Speak to yourself with honesty, pride, and kindness.

When Reframing Isn't Enough

Sometimes, cognitive shifts don't work right away—especially when trauma, OCD, or deeply rooted beliefs are involved. That's okay. In these moments, mindfulness and exposure work may be more effective than forcing a new thought.

You also don't have to go it alone. A skilled therapist can help you explore and transform those deeper patterns with support and safety.

Integration Practice

Try this CBT thought log:

- ❖ Situation: "I made a mistake at work."
- ❖ Thought: "I'm a failure."
- ❖ Feeling: "Ashamed, anxious."
- ❖ New Thought: "Everyone makes mistakes. I can learn from this."
- ❖ New Feeling: "Relieved, more hopeful."

Affirmations

Use for a Healthy Mindset Choose one or two of these to repeat during your morning routine or in moments of stress. Let them anchor you into a mindset of curiosity, self-compassion, and growth.

- ❖ I am not my thoughts.
- ❖ My thoughts are powerful, and I can choose them.

- ❖ I let go of the need to be perfect.
- ❖ I am learning, growing, and evolving.
- ❖ I see myself and others through the eyes of compassion.

Small shifts make a big difference over time. Be curious. Be kind. And trust that change is possible—one thought at a time.

Journal Prompts

1. What stories have I been telling myself about who I am or what I'm capable of? Where did they come from?
2. Which thought patterns tend to keep me stuck or small? How do they show up in my daily life?
3. What is one belief I'm ready to release—and what belief would I like to replace it with?
4. What evidence do I have that contradicts the negative thoughts I often believe?
5. When I speak to myself, is my tone more like a critic or a compassionate friend? What would I say to a loved one going through what I am?
6. What does my "inner bully" often say—and what is the truth I want to begin speaking instead?
7. How would my life feel if I fully believed I am enough, just as I am?

CHAPTER 7

Feel it to Heal it — How to Do the Work in Real Life

"When we allow ourselves to feel, we begin to heal."

— *Kim McMillen*

This chapter is all about feeling to heal. It's about choosing to face the uncomfortable emotions we've spent years running from and learning to be with them instead of pushing them away.

A common fear that many people share is: "If I let myself feel this, the floodgates will open and never close."

That fear makes sense. Most of us were never taught how to feel our emotions. We were taught to distract, suppress, or numb. But the truth is: all emotions are temporary. When we allow ourselves to feel them fully, they move through us. What keeps them stuck is our resistance.

One evening, I was driving home after visiting friends in my old hometown. I left early because I had a meditation retreat to lead the next morning. As I was driving home, I felt sadness and loneliness creep in. A bit of FOMO, too. In the past, I would've pushed those feelings away—kept myself busy or distracted to avoid them. But on this day, I chose differently.

I labeled the emotions. I let myself feel them. Within five minutes, they had passed, just like that.

And I felt proud. Because that small moment showed me how much I had grown. It reminded me that feeling my feelings is safe and that I can let my emotions move through without them taking over.

Now, of course, that's an example of a relatively light emotion. Bigger emotions take more time. More space. But the process is the same.

I remember working at a men's prison early in my career. I had only been a therapist for about six months when I met a client who had just lost his mother. He was completely devastated. Struggling to manage his emotions. Desperate for medication to numb the pain.

This was before I had discovered mindfulness. I tried all the coping skills I had been taught—but nothing worked.

Eventually, in my desperation to support him, I spoke to the psychiatrist. I asked if he could see the client sooner.

Facing Emotional Resistance

What he said to me changed everything. "Miss Weimer, some emotions have to be felt to pass. He doesn't need medication right now. He needs to grieve. That's how he will get better."

I felt a little embarrassed that I hadn't thought of that myself. But he was absolutely right. That conversation planted a seed in me—a seed that would grow into one of my core beliefs: we must feel it to heal it.

We live in a world that glorifies avoiding discomfort. But true healing comes when we stop running. The next time you feel triggered, overwhelmed, or heavy—try this:

1. Name the emotion. Put language to it. "I'm feeling sad." "I'm feeling anxious." "I'm feeling angry."
2. Notice where it lives in your body. Is your chest tight? Your stomach turning? Your jaw clenched?
3. Breathe into it. Inhale gently. Exhale slowly. Make space for the sensation.
4. Allow it to be there. Don't rush it. Don't force it away. Just be with it.

5. Stay present. Trust that the emotion will pass—as all emotions do.
6. Express it. Deeper emotions often require more intentional processing. Journaling can be incredibly helpful. Call a supportive friend. Talk with a therapist or coach. Choose what works for you, but don't keep it bottled up—give your emotions a safe place to land.

Moving Emotions Through the Body

This is what real shadow work looks like. It's not about going on a retreat or diving into your childhood every weekend. It's about choosing, moment by moment, to stay with yourself, especially when it's hard.

The more we practice this, the more our body learns that it is safe to feel. That we won't abandon ourselves. That we can stay rooted even in the storms.

Emotions are not problems to fix. They are messengers. Invitations. They show us where love and healing are needed most.

And when we stop pushing them away, we find something extraordinary: that under the pain, there is wisdom. There is resilience. And there is light.

Feel it. Heal it. Free yourself.

Creating Space to Feel

Creating space to feel means slowing down enough to listen to what your body, heart, and inner world are trying to say. It's about pausing before you push away the discomfort, softening into the moment instead of bracing against it.

In our fast-paced world, we're taught to move on, distract, or fix—but healing begins when we give ourselves permission to just feel. This doesn't require hours of solitude or dramatic expression.

Sometimes, it's simply placing a hand on your heart, closing your eyes, and saying, "I'm here."

Sometimes, we need to take time to journal all of our thoughts and feelings about something that has happened. It is not uncommon for us to have multiple emotions about things or to feel numb and have no idea what you feel. That is okay! Sit with, journal, and talk with a friend or a therapist about it. What is most important is that you create the space to allow yourself to feel what you need to feel until there is nothing left to feel!

When we create intentional space—through breath, stillness, or gentle movement—we send a signal to the nervous system that it's safe to release. Emotion is energy in motion. When we create room for it to move through us, we free ourselves from what once felt too heavy to carry.

Affirmations

Use these affirmations as daily anchors or repeat them silently when navigating emotional waves:

- ❖ I create space for my emotions without judgment.
- ❖ It is safe for me to feel everything I feel.
- ❖ My emotions are messengers, not enemies.
- ❖ I trust the wisdom of my body and the rhythm of my healing.
- ❖ I allow myself to soften instead of suppress.
- ❖ Every emotion I welcome brings me closer to wholeness.
- ❖ I am no longer afraid of my own inner world.
- ❖ The feeling is not a weakness—it is my path to freedom.
- ❖ I am here, present, and open to what arises.

Journal Prompts

You are encouraged to explore their inner landscape gently and honestly:

1. What emotions do I most often avoid, and why?
2. What was I taught about expressing feelings as a child?
3. What would it feel like to fully allow an emotion without needing to change it?
4. When was the last time I gave myself permission to cry, scream, laugh, or rest? What did I notice?
5. What physical sensations do I notice when I feel overwhelmed, and what might those sensations be telling me?
6. If my emotions had a voice, what would they want to say to me today?
7. What can I do to create more safety and space in my life to feel deeply?
8. How does my body respond when I choose to feel instead of fix?

CHAPTER 8

Healing the Child Within

"Nurturing your inner child unlocks the door to your deepest healing."

— ***Kimberly Weimer***

Much of what we do in adulthood is shaped by the beliefs, fears, and experiences—both good and painful—that we carried with us from childhood. Whether we realize it or not, our inner child often plays a quiet but powerful role in our thoughts, behaviors, and relationships. Until we acknowledge and care for that part of ourselves, we may continue to react to life from a place of wounding rather than from our highest self.

I didn't have a great childhood. And while I've spoken about this in earlier chapters, what I've come to understand through my own healing is that the environment I grew up in taught me to control, over-function, and caretake in order to feel safe. I learned to stay hyper-aware of others' moods, to manage their emotions before my own, and to prioritize peace at any cost—even if it meant abandoning myself.

As an adult, I found myself making impulsive decisions in search of connection, joy, or a moment of peace. Many of those decisions led to pain. On the surface, I wanted love and security—but underneath, I was unconsciously projecting the energy of a little girl who didn't feel worthy of being protected or cherished. That energy attracted relationships and experiences that reinforced the wounds I hadn't yet healed.

Meeting the Inner Child

Everything began to shift when I realized what was truly happening. I wasn't broken—I was unmothered. I was unprotected. I was never taught to nurture or soothe myself. And the most important work I could do wasn't to "fix" myself—it was to re-parent myself.

Reconnecting With Needs

I began doing inner child meditations. I started journaling, asking that younger version of me what she needed. I listened. I cried. And I responded with love.

Practicing Inner Nurturing

When she told me she was tired, I let her rest. When she needed nurturing, I wrapped myself in a blanket, cooked comforting meals, or laid on the earth and let the sun warm my skin. When she needed to play, I danced around the living room to my favorite music. When she needed love, I looked in the mirror and said, "I love you."

It became a daily conversation. A gentle, loving ritual. I'd ask, "Okay, baby girl, what do you need right now?" And I'd honor her needs.

This practice changed everything. I no longer ignored my own discomfort or pushed through pain the way I once had. I began to recognize when the little girl inside me felt overwhelmed, or when she wanted to hide, or when she needed reassurance—and I started offering her the very things she had gone without.

What Is Inner Child Work?

Inner child work is the practice of connecting with and healing the wounded parts of yourself that formed in childhood. It's a way of re-parenting yourself—offering your inner child the safety, love, and nurturing that may have been missing when you were young.

We all carry parts of ourselves from the past: the scared one, the playful one, the one who was told to sit down and be quiet, the one who never felt good enough, the one who had to grow up too fast. Inner child work helps us understand where our patterns and emotional reactions come from, and it gives us tools to heal those tender places.

How to Begin Inner Child Work

Here are a few ways to begin gently reconnecting with your inner child:

- ❖ **Inner child journaling:** Write a letter to your younger self. Ask how they're feeling. Ask what they need. Let them respond through your pen. Don't overthink it—let it flow.

- ❖ **Guided meditations:** There are many beautiful inner child meditations available online that help you visualize meeting and nurturing your younger self. This can be incredibly powerful, especially when done regularly.

- ❖ **Daily check-ins:** Simply pause and ask, "What does my inner child need right now?" Then respond lovingly—whether that's taking a break, saying no, eating a nourishing meal, or doing something joyful.

- ❖ **Self-soothing rituals:** Create nurturing practices for yourself. Wrap up in a soft blanket, drink a warm cup of tea, cuddle with a pet, listen to music that makes you feel safe, or take a bath with essential oils.

❖ **Speak lovingly to yourself**: Look in the mirror and say kind things. Speak to yourself the way you would speak to a small child who just wants to be loved.

Inner child work is not about dwelling in the past—it's about reclaiming the parts of yourself that got left behind. It's about giving yourself the love and support you always deserved.

You are not too much. You are not too needy. You are not broken. You are a tender soul learning to love all of yourself.

And your inner child has been waiting for you.

Let this chapter be your invitation to meet them—and to welcome them home.

Affirmations

Read aloud or write them down daily to anchor your healing intention.

- ❖ I am safe to meet all parts of myself with compassion.
- ❖ My inner child is worthy of love, safety, and joy.
- ❖ I give myself permission to feel, to rest, and to play.
- ❖ I honor my past without letting it define my future.
- ❖ I am learning to re-parent myself with kindness and care.
- ❖ I am no longer abandoning myself—I am here, I am present.
- ❖ I am healing, gently and completely, one breath at a time.

Journal Prompts

Use these to reconnect with your younger self and explore how early experiences shaped your present self.

1. When do I feel most connected to my inner child? What am I doing in those moments?
2. What messages did I receive as a child about love, safety, or worthiness? How do they still impact me today?
3. What did I need as a child that I didn't receive? How can I give that to myself now?
4. If my inner child could speak to me today, what would they say? What do they need to hear from me?
5. What small rituals or acts of care can I create to nurture the child within me each day?

CHAPTER 9

Befriending Anxiety and Fear — Learning to Lean In

"Fear is a natural reaction to moving closer to the truth."

— *Pema Chödrön*

Shifting the Fear Narrative

Anxiety and fear feel like the enemies of peace—but they don't have to be. What if, instead of resisting them, we learned to lean in?

One of the most powerful lessons I've learned is that fear is not the enemy—it's the invitation. It's the voice saying, "There's something here to be seen, something to be healed."

When we avoid what we fear, we strengthen its hold. The brain learns that whatever we're avoiding must be dangerous. But when we gently lean in, we teach the brain something new: "I can do this. I can survive this. I am safe."

Embracing Exposure Work

At first, this work can feel completely counterintuitive.

I can't tell you how many times a client has looked at me and said, "Kim, you want me to intentionally trigger a panic attack… to heal my panic attacks?"

And my answer is always the same: Absolutely YES.

Let me explain why.

Imagine you're terrified of snakes. If we were working together, we wouldn't just throw you into a room full of snakes. We'd create a hierarchy of fears— starting small and building up gradually. First, you'd simply look at a photo of a snake. Then, when that felt manageable, you might watch a video of one. Later, you'd visit a pet store and observe a snake from a distance.

Eventually, maybe—maybe—you'd be able to hold one.

Will your brain ever love snakes? Probably not. But it will learn an essential truth: being near a snake doesn't mean certain death. You can be around what you fear and survive.

Now, thoughts and emotions aren't physical like snakes—but we can use the exact same concept.

We create a hierarchy of fear—starting with the least triggering scenarios and working our way up. We intentionally face the fear, sit with the discomfort, and allow it to rise and fall without escaping or trying to fix it. And with time, your brain learns: this is uncomfortable, but it's not dangerous.

Let me give you a real example.

I've worked with many clients who were paralyzed by a fear of making mistakes. For them, it wasn't just a small worry—it was black-and-white thinking: either they were perfect, or they were a complete failure.

Many of them struggled even to send an important email. They would agonize over every word, reread it twenty times, and still be terrified of hitting "send."

So, we started small.

First, I had them imagine sending an email with a glaring error.

Next, they pictured their worst-case scenario: their boss publicly shaming them at a meeting, co-workers laughing behind their backs. We sat with the anxiety— no distraction, no "fixing"—until the wave of fear naturally rose and fell.

When they could tolerate the imagined fear, we moved to real-world practice.

I asked them to write a pretend email with an intentional (but harmless) mistake and send it to themselves.

Then, once that became manageable, we leveled up: they would send an actual work email with a small, hidden error—while holding space for all the "what-ifs" running wild in their mind.

To keep them from spiraling, we added limits: only two quick proofs before sending. Strict time caps. No endless obsessing.

And you know what?

Over time, sending emails—even imperfect ones—became easier. The anxiety shrank because they stopped reinforcing the fear through avoidance.

This approach may sound silly at first. But for people stuck in perfectionism, overthinking, and fear of judgment, it's life-changing.

I use this technique—called Exposure Response Prevention (ERP)— with all my clients who struggle with specific fears, anxiety, or obsessive thoughts.

As backward as it may seem, the only way to heal from fear isn't to run from it.

It's to walk straight through it—with compassion, courage, and support.

This is the foundation of what's known as exposure work in therapeutic practice. The concept is simple: instead of avoiding what scares us, we move toward it—gradually, compassionately, and consistently—until it no longer controls us.

That thing you're afraid of? That thought you're running from? When you turn toward it, sit with it, breathe into it—something shifts.

Let's say the thought is: "They probably hate me."

Instead of challenging the thought, what if you agreed with it?

"Yes, they might hate me. They might think I'm strange or weird or too much. Maybe they do." Sit with all the scenarios in your head and assume maybe they are true. Your anxiety will rise, but in time, it will also fall. The more times you do this, the more your brain and body accept this as just another thought that will come and pass. You no longer have to fear it because it is just another thought.

And then... you allow yourself to feel the discomfort that thought brings up. You breathe. You stay. You let it rise. And eventually—it passes.

This is where mindfulness is so important. You're not feeding the fear. You're not fueling the story. You're simply noticing the thought, feeling the feeling, and letting it move through you.

Over time, the thought loses power. The brain stops reacting so intensely. The nervous system learns, "This is uncomfortable, but it's not dangerous."

This is the heart of healing anxiety. And it requires presence, patience, and practice.

Disrupting the Panic Cycle

As someone who has struggled with anxiety and specializes in anxiety disorders—particularly OCD—I've lived this work both professionally and personally. Throughout my life, I've struggled with panic disorder and obsessive-compulsive tendencies. I tried all the coping strategies taught to me in school: breathing exercises, grounding, distraction, tapping, and challenging thoughts. These helped in the short term, but the panic always came back. Breathing would slow my heart rate temporarily, and grounding would bring me back for a moment—but the cycle repeated itself.

When I discovered Exposure Response Prevention (ERP), everything changed. I realized that when anxiety begins, it triggers a physical response—racing heart, dizziness, shortness of breath. We then panic about those sensations, which causes more anxiety, more symptoms, and more panic. It becomes a loop.

So, I made a conscious decision to break that cycle.

Instead of trying to calm down, I did something radical: I felt the anxiety on purpose. I sat with it. I labeled the sensations. "My heart is racing—that's my anxiety. I feel dizzy—that's anxiety. It's hard to breathe—this is anxiety."

The first time I did this, the anxiety passed in about 20 minutes—much shorter than my usual panic episodes. The second time, it took 10 minutes. Eventually, I stopped having panic attacks altogether. Do I still get anxious? Absolutely. But now, when I notice it rising, I sit with it and allow it. My brain seems to say, "You're no fun. Never mind. No panic attack for you."

I've taught this to hundreds of clients over the years, and I've watched it transform lives. It's not easy work—but it is powerful. ERP and mindfulness are not about avoiding symptoms or trying to fix them. They're about changing your relationship with anxiety, learning to sit with it, and letting it pass without needing to control it.

And yes—it works.

Applying Mindful Courage

When fear arises, try this approach:

1. Name the fear. Bring it into conscious awareness. "I'm afraid of being judged."
2. Agree with the thought. Don't fight it. Say, "Yes, that might be true. They are judging me."
3. Feel the feeling. Let the anxiety rise. Notice the physical sensations. Stay with it.
4. Observe and allow. Anchor yourself in the moment without reassuring yourself. Just be present!
5. Let it pass. Don't force it. Trust the wave to rise and fall.

Many clients tell me, "If I let myself go there, I'll spiral out of control." But here's what actually happens: when you stop resisting the emotion, it usually passes much faster than you expect.

Anxiety Cycle Explained

Here's the truth:

The more you fight anxiety, the worse it gets.

Let me explain why.

Anxiety operates through a feedback loop.

First, stress triggers a hormone release—like adrenaline and cortisol— which ramps up the sensations of anxiety: racing heart, tight chest, shaky hands, and shortness of breath.

Then, because those physical sensations feel scary, you panic about being anxious.

Guess what happens next?

Your body releases even more stress hormones, making the anxiety feel even stronger.

The more you freak out about feeling anxious, the more your body fuels the fire.

It's a vicious cycle—but the good news is: you can break it.

How?

By sitting with the anxiety.

By allowing it to rise... and fall... without trying to push it away.

I know it feels terrifying.

Panic sensations feel like you're dying.

But in the immortal words of *The Hangover Part II:*

"But did you die?"

The answer is always no.

It's scary as hell—but you survived just fine. And you'll survive this, too. Here's another way I often explain it:

Think about when you go for a hard run or a tough workout. What happens in your body?

- ❖ Heart pounding
- ❖ Chest tightening
- ❖ Breathing hard
- ❖ Feeling dizzy or shaky

Now, think about a panic attack. Same exact symptoms.

But when you're working out, you feel proud. You celebrate the effort.

You don't spiral—you think, "Wow, I'm getting stronger."

Yet when those same sensations come from anxiety, your brain immediately sounds the alarm:

"Danger! Something's wrong!"

Same body.

Same sensations.

Completely different story.

Next time you feel panic starting to rise, try this simple sequence:

1. Stop. Feel the sensations in your body. No judgment.
2. Label it. Gently say to yourself: "This is anxiety. That's all it is."
3. Allow. Keep feeling the sensations without trying to fix them. Stay curious and compassionate.
4. Ride it out. Trust that the wave will rise... and it will fall.

Over time, your brain will learn:

"I can survive this. I don't have to run from it."

One of my favorite mantras to share with clients is:

"You have to feel it to heal it."

And when it comes to fear, I'll add:

"You have to face it to free yourself."

But remember: you don't have to dive headfirst into your biggest fear all at once.

Healing happens layer by layer. Start small.

Be gentle.

Stay consistent.

You are stronger than your fear—and with each moment of allowing instead of fighting, you're teaching your mind and body:

"I am safe. I am capable. I am free." Speak Your Fear Out Loud!

There's a powerful example of this idea in the show This Is Us. In several episodes, when something scary or overwhelming happens, Randall and his wife pause, look at each other, and ask, "What are you most afraid of?" They speak their worst fears aloud. And just like that, some of the fear loses its grip. Saying it out loud can be the support we need. Often, when we name our fears, we realize they're not as overwhelming as they seemed. Speaking out loud takes away their power. And if that doesn't work—if the fear still lingers—sit with it a little longer. It will pass. I promise.

Start Small and Build a Foundation

Choose manageable exposures. And if it feels like too much, work with a trained ERP or mindfulness-based therapist. You don't have to do it alone.

But do the work. Don't let fear rule your life.

Because fear isn't here to paralyze you, it's here to teach you. To show you what matters. To call you toward growth.

When we lean into our fear, we reclaim our power. We stop running. We stop avoiding it. And we step into courage—one breath at a time.

Affirmations

- I am safe to feel discomfort and move through it with grace.
- Fear is not my enemy—it is a messenger.
- I am capable of sitting with uncertainty.
- Each time I face my fear, I reclaim my power.
- I trust my body to guide me through anxiety.
- I do not need to control everything to feel at peace.
- My courage is greater than my fear.
- I am learning to lean in, not run away.
- I am grounded, present, and resilient.

Journal Prompts

1. What am I currently avoiding because of fear or anxiety?
2. What does my fear want me to know or protect me from?
3. What happens when I sit with fear instead of running from it?
4. How has anxiety tried to protect me in the past? Is that protection still needed?

5. Write about a time you faced a fear and came out stronger. What helped you through it?

6. What would it look like to gently lean into discomfort instead of avoiding it?

7. If my anxiety had a voice, what would it say—and what would I say back with compassion?

CHAPTER 10

The Art of Surrender — Letting Go and Trusting the Process

"Surrender is the inner transition from resistance to acceptance—from no to yes."

— *Eckhart Tolle*

Surrender is one of the most misunderstood but powerful aspects of healing. It doesn't mean giving up or becoming passive. It means loosening your grip on how you think things should be, and instead allowing life to unfold with trust. In time, you learn that all of this beautiful life we live is filled with lessons and growth that bring us closer to unconditional love and peace! We get there easier when we surrender to the process.

Releasing the Need for Control

Our anxious brains love control. We want plans, timelines, and guarantees. We obsess over "what ifs," and our minds create endless backup plans for backup plans. But here's what I've noticed—not just in my clients, but in myself: 99.9% of the things we fear never actually happen. Most of the time, life unfolds more smoothly than we expect. And when something does go wrong? It's rarely what we feared—and we still find a way through it.

We torture ourselves over and over, spending so much energy trying to predict and prevent every problem that we miss out on the beauty right in front of us. We miss moments of connection, joy, and peace because we're wrapped up in future scenarios that may never come. We are wasting our beautiful lives in our tortured minds, thinking we can predict and control the future.

One phrase I use with clients all the time is: "I'll cross that bridge if or when I come to it." It's become a mantra in my own life. When a worry pops up, I ask:

1. Can I do something about this right now or in the next few days?
2. If yes—do it. If no—
3. Can I do something about it in the next few months?
4. If yes, schedule it.
5. If not, imagine placing it in a box, wrapping it with a bow, and putting it on a high shelf in the back of your mind. Every time this thought comes back up, do this process again!

This simple act of symbolic release helps the mind let go. And it makes space for peace.

Listening to Spirit

I remember a time when surrender showed up in a very tangible way. I was newly divorced, raising two teenage boys with very little support. I had been saving for a vacation—something special for us. Every time I got close to having enough money, something would break. The AC went out. A pothole blew my tire and destroyed my rim. Then, the radiator failed. Each time, I dipped into the trip savings. Finally, the last straw: the washing machine stopped working. I had no money left to fix it.

I threw my hands in the air and said, "Okay, Spirit, I can't fix this. It's up to you."

Later that afternoon, as I was filling a glass of water in the kitchen, I heard that familiar nudge from Spirit: "Try it now." I walked over, pressed the button, and the washing machine started right up.

Not only that—but later that evening, I was nudged again. "Check your mail." I had ignored the mail for months, but when I did, I found several checks I hadn't opened. They added up to more than what I needed for the trip.

That night in meditation, I heard: "Had you not been saving for the trip, you wouldn't have had money for the repairs. I was teaching you that even when things aren't going your way, I have a plan. I am taking care of you."

That experience shifted everything. I learned that surrender doesn't mean giving up—it means trusting that even when things don't make sense, they're still unfolding for your good.

Years later, I read The Surrender Experiment by Michael A. Singer. In it, he shares his story of giving up control and allowing Spirit to guide his life. The blessings he received—and the lessons he learned—were extraordinary.

That book confirmed my many lessons on surrender: when we let go of the grip, we make room for miracles.

Trusting the Unseen Path

Around that time, I stopped trying to force things. I let go of relationships that weren't aligned, and I watched new friendships blossom—my soul tribe. My business began to grow. I found my voice on social media. This book began to take shape. Were parts of that journey painful? Yes. Was it scary to step into the unknown? Absolutely. But was it worth it? A thousand times, yes.

Practicing Daily Surrender

Surrender is not a one-time event. It's a practice. A choice we make daily. To trust. To release. To align with what's unfolding rather than fight it.

You may also find it helpful to set the tone for your day with affirmations that support a surrendered mindset. Choose one or two that resonate and repeat them slowly while breathing deeply:

❖ I trust the timing of my life.

- ❖ I am safe to let go of control.
- ❖ Spirit is guiding me always.
- ❖ I release what no longer serves me.
- ❖ I am held and supported by something greater.
- ❖ I surrender my expectations and embrace what is.
- ❖ I let go of resistance and welcome peace.
- ❖ I choose faith over fear.
- ❖ I am open to receiving what is meant for me.
- ❖ I allow life to unfold with grace and ease.

These affirmations, when practiced regularly, help rewire the mind for trust, openness, and presence.

You don't have to figure it all out. You don't need all the answers. You just need presence, intention, and faith.

Surrender isn't a weakness. It's wisdom. It's trust in the timing, the unfolding, and the deeper plan that is always guiding you home.

It is remembering when one door closes, another is opening that is better for you.

It is remembering that if something is not working out is either a redirection or protection. When I was a kid, I rode horses competitively. We often traveled early in the morning to get to horse shows. One morning, it seemed like everything was going wrong. The truck battery was dead, and then the horse that always excitedly jumped in the trailer refused to get in. We were almost an hour late by the time we got on the road. After being on the road for 45 minutes in the famous Tule fog, we were at a dead stop. We heard on the news that there had been a huge pile-up on the road about 30 minutes earlier. There were many and many deaths/injuries. Had we left on time, we would have been in the middle of that accident. Spirit was protecting us by creating chaos. Though we left the house that morning frustrated, we settled into gratitude as we realized we were being divinely protected! I learned at that young age that sometimes the frustrations in life are actually blessings meant to redirect us to something better and protect us from something meant to harm us.

Although some look at surrender as weak, it is actually the complete opposite of weakness. We control from a place of fear. We surrender from a place of peace, faith, and knowing that all things work together for our greater good. Though surrender brings deep freedom in the long run, it takes incredible faith and self-discipline to truly let go and allow life to unfold. Looking back, I can see that I've forced a lot of things in my life. If I wanted something, I could usually make it happen—through pushing, working, pleading, and striving. But often, the things I forced ended up bringing me more stress or unhappiness than joy.

In more recent years, as I've practiced letting go and learning to trust Spirit to lead me, I can't help but wonder how different things might have been if I had surrendered sooner. Maybe I would have experienced a more peaceful marriage, earlier success, or an easier path. Or maybe—just maybe—I was meant to walk every twist and turn to gather the wisdom I now carry.

I may never know for sure. But what I do know is this: I'm grateful. For all of it. Every hardship has taught me something. Every moment of surrender has strengthened my faith. And I've been able to use those lessons to help others—an incredible gift and honor.

Each day, I learn a little more. I soften a little more. I trust a little more. And the more I practice this, the more I realize: the Universe truly does have my back. I don't have to grasp and control. I can sit back, breathe, and allow.

There's a mindfulness teaching that says: "The quickest path to disappointment is expectation." When we cling to how we think things should unfold, we set ourselves up for frustration and missed opportunities. Worse, we might even be resisting something far greater that Spirit had planned for us.

When we release our grip and simply show up as our best selves—fully present, growing, and open—we make room for miracles. We create space for peace, for joy, and for blessings far beyond what we ever imagined.

Surrender isn't a one-time act. It's a way of living. A way of trusting. A way of receiving.

Affirmations:

- ❖ I trust the timing of my life.
- ❖ I am safe to let go of control.
- ❖ Spirit is guiding me always.
- ❖ I release what no longer serves me.
- ❖ I am Divinely held and guided.
- ❖ I surrender my expectations and embrace what is.
- ❖ I let go of resistance and welcome peace.
- ❖ I choose faith over fear.
- ❖ I am open to receiving what is meant for me.
- ❖ I allow life to unfold with grace and ease.

Journal Prompts:

1. What am I currently trying to control that may be asking to be released?
2. Where in my life am I being invited to trust more deeply?
3. What would it feel like to fully surrender this situation to Spirit or the Universe?
4. When have things worked out better than I imagined, even when I didn't have a plan?
5. What fears arise when I think about letting go—and what might be underneath those fears?

6. What signs, synchronicities, or inner nudges have shown up recently that I haven't fully trusted?

7. If I believed with my whole heart that life was unfolding for me, what would I do differently today?

8. What does "surrender" look like in real, tangible ways in my daily life?

9. How can I create more space for stillness, silence, or prayer to support my surrender practice?

10. Write a letter to your higher self or Spirit: What do you need help surrendering right now? What guidance are you ready to receive?

CHAPTER 11

Living in Flow — Aligning with Spirit's Guidance

"Spirit speaks in whispers, in nudges, in the pull of the current—flow is found when you listen."

— *Kim Weimer*

Understanding Flow State

Flow happens when we stop trying to force life to happen and instead learn to dance with what is. It's the art of listening inward, trusting our intuition, and staying grounded as life unfolds around us. This chapter is about staying open to what Spirit brings, even when it's unexpected, and learning how to support ourselves energetically and emotionally as we grow.

I was hiking recently with friends, and we reached the top of a hill overlooking a river. It was spring—the snow was melting, and the river was high, twisting with strong currents and rapids. We paused to meditate, soaking in the magic of the mountains and water. I found myself drawn to the river. Spirit began to speak to me about flow.

I observed the river carving through the rocks—how it moved over, around, and even into obstacles in its path. There were peaceful stretches, dangerous rapids, and curves that disappeared from view. Spirit reminded me that life is like this river. We can't always see what's coming. There are calm seasons and chaotic ones. Sometimes, it feels like we're smashing into boulders or stuck in relentless rapids. It can feel like we are lost, but we always find our way back!

Don't Fight the Current

I often go white water rafting. They teach us: if you fall out of the boat, lie on your back, feet pointed downstream, and float. Let the water carry you until the boat can pick you up. Life is like that. The more we fight the current, the more energy we waste. When we surrender and flow with it— trusting Spirit to guide or rescue us when needed—everything gets easier. If a door closes, look for another to open. Spirit often sends us little nudges in the right direction. If we are paying attention we will see the path. If things feel off or hard, maybe that is a clue that you are working too hard?

Look for ways to return to flow.

Reclaiming Your Energy

One of the most powerful ways I've learned to live in flow is by starting each day with meditation and intention-setting practice. It's a cornerstone in my life—a way to protect my energy and reconnect with what matters.

My morning ritual begins with simply sitting and breathing. I visualize breathing in what I want to embody—peace, clarity, strength—and exhaling what no longer serves me: stress, anxiety, or my busy monkey mind.

Then, I imagine a whirlwind of light spiraling down from the top of my head, clearing anything that doesn't belong. I don't need to name it—Spirit knows. I release it with love.

Next, I call my energy back to me. So often, we leave parts of ourselves scattered in conversations, worries, or past events. I lovingly return others' energy to them, wrapped in light.

I visualize roots growing deep into the earth, anchoring and stabilizing me. I draw up Earth's nurturing energy, releasing what's heavy and receiving love and light in return.

Then, I imagine a glowing light inside me—starting wherever it feels strongest.

It grows and expands, wrapping around me like a protective bubble. Only love and light can come in. Only love and light can go out.

With that energy in place, I place the tip of my tongue on the roof of my mouth, take a deep breath, and set my intention for the day. Some days, it's love and light. Other days, it's surrender, alignment, presence, or trust. I let my intuition choose.

Staying Focused on Your Intentions

You can support your intention throughout the day with reminders. Set phone alarms. Use sticky notes on your mirror or desk. Or simply pause and take three grounding breaths. This isn't about perfection. It's about presence.

Speaking the Language of Flow

Living in flow also means being willing to release what no longer aligns. That might be a job, a belief, a relationship, or an outdated version of yourself. When you trust Spirit's gentle nudges and stay aligned with your values, life begins to organize itself around your peace.

Sometimes, we resist the very things that would set us free. But when we live in flow, we trust that if something falls away, something better is on the way. And if something arrives unexpectedly, it may be exactly what we needed.

Stay grounded. Stay present. Keep listening.

When you live in flow, you don't have to force the path. You become the path—allowing Spirit to guide and provide you with blessings you didn't even know were possible.

Affirmations for Flow

Here are a few gentle affirmations to help anchor your energy in flow:

- ❖ I trust the timing of my life.
- ❖ I flow with what life brings.
- ❖ I let go of resistance and allow Spirit to guide me.
- ❖ I release control and embrace ease.
- ❖ I am aligned with love, peace, and truth.
- ❖ I move with grace through the twists and turns.
- ❖ I am grounded, centered, and in harmony with all that is.
- ❖ I surrender my need to know what's next.
- ❖ I make space for miracles.
- ❖ I live in trust and flow.

Repeat these to yourself in the morning or anytime you feel stuck or overwhelmed. Let them be gentle reminders that you're always supported—and that the current is leading you exactly where you're meant to go.

Journal Prompts

1. Where in my life am I currently forcing instead of flowing? What would it feel like to release control in that area?
2. When have I felt most "in flow" with life? What was I doing, and how can I cultivate more of that energy now?
3. What nudges or whispers from Spirit have I been ignoring? What might they be guiding me toward?
4. How do I know when I am aligned with my highest self? What are the signs in my body, mind, or surroundings?

5. If I fully trusted Spirit to guide me today, what decision or action would I take differently?

6. What energy do I want to embody more consistently—peace, joy, trust, creativity, love? How can I start my mornings with the intention to invite that in?

7. What fears keep me from surrendering more fully to life's unfolding? What affirmations or truths help me soften those fears?

CHAPTER 12

The Freedom of Forgiveness — Releasing the Weight We Carry

"Holding onto anger is like drinking poison and expecting the other person to die."

*— **Buddha (attributed)***

Forgiveness is not about condoning what happened or letting someone off the hook. It's about freeing yourself from the pain that keeps you tied to the past. It's about letting go of the energetic weight of resentment, anger, guilt, and shame—not for them, but for you. I'm going to repeat that: It is not about them; it is 100% about you!

When we hold on to anger or hurt, it doesn't just live in our minds—it settles into our bodies. The tension in our shoulders, the clenching in our jaws, the unease in our stomachs—these are all signals from the body that something emotional is asking to be acknowledged and released.

Suppressed emotions can lead to chronic stress, anxiety, depression, and even physical illness. Forgiveness, by contrast, supports nervous system regulation, emotional balance, and overall well-being.

The Mind-Body Connection of Unforgiveness

Our bodies remember. When we carry anger or pain, our nervous system can stay stuck in survival mode: fight, flight, or freeze. This chronic state can disrupt sleep, digestion, immune function, and energy levels.

Forgiveness helps break this cycle. It tells the body, "We are safe now." It allows the nervous system to soften, restore, and heal.

Letting Go to Lighten the Load

Let me give you a personal example of this. For many years, I had rock-hard knots in my shoulders. I got weekly massages, stretched, iced, heated, took medications, I tried everything to get them to release. Nothing worked! I read Louise Hays' book You Can Heal Your Life. The book has ailments with causes and affirmations to shift what is going on in the body. I looked up shoulder pain, and it was related to anger and boy, could I relate to that. I was a supervisor of one of the largest mental health programs in the state, and almost every hour, something frustrating or stupid would happen. I'm not proud of this, but staff often heard profanities from my office as I attempted to manage the chaos that was constantly happening at that time. Under my name on my door was the title Chaos Coordinator because that is what I felt like I did 90% of my day! After reading that my pain was linked to the anger and frustration I was holding onto at work, I decided to make a huge change. I decided to respond in peace and love as much as I could. I started meditating on love before work. I set timers, reminding myself to return to love and peace. I posted pictures in my office with inspiring quotes about love and light. I did everything I could think of to keep this in my mind throughout my day. At the start of this, my massage therapist apartment burned down, and she had a baby. It was almost a year before she got back to work. As I laid on her table, she was like what in the world happened to your body. It is completely different. The once rock-solid knots in my back were now moving and starting to loosen up. I had not had a single massage since her. I hadn't changed anything else.

The only change was my choice to remain in love and let go of anger! I actively worked on sending light to the angry, unforgiven places in my life and allowed things to be what they were going to be without being angry about it. This changed everything in my body!

Letting go of Victim Mentality

Spirit's Lessons on Forgiveness and Owning My Story

In the past few years, Spirit has taught me some of my biggest lessons— especially about forgiveness and how identifying as a victim was silently holding me back.

As I shared earlier in this book, my childhood was tough at times, and my marriage was even harder to manage. For many years, I carried deep anger toward my mom and my husband for "the abuse they put me through."

And to be fair—especially as a child—I had very little control over what was happening around me. But as an adult, I had choices. And some of those choices kept me stuck.

Even coming home from my honeymoon, I knew in my gut that I had made a huge mistake.

Just a few months in, when the loud, aggressive outbursts started over the smallest things, I saw the red flags—but I stayed.

I chose to abandon myself in the hope of making him happy.

I chose to walk on eggshells, placating him at every turn, hoping that somehow things would magically get better.

When I finally escaped that marriage, I clung to my identity as the victim. I blamed my mother's behavior for shaping me into someone who would choose a man like that.

And while from a psychological perspective, that's understandable, it didn't absolve me from taking responsibility for the choices I continued to make.

When Spirit confronted me with this truth, I'm not going to lie—I was furious.

I didn't want to own my part.

I had worn the "survivor" badge like armor: *Look what I lived through. Look how strong I am for succeeding anyway!*

On a deeper shadow level, I craved the compassion and praise I received when people acknowledged my struggles.

Compassion. Connection. Validation.

All the things I didn't get much of as a child.

But here's the cost:

As long as I needed to be seen as the victim, I stayed stuck as the victim.

When we over-identify with a past wound, we unconsciously keep living in that role—and continue attracting the same painful patterns.

It took serious self-reflection, deep inner work, hypnosis, and challenging my thoughts every time they slid back into "poor me" territory to finally shift. Letting go of the victim story wasn't about blaming myself—it was about reclaiming my power.

It meant forgiving myself:

- ❖ For all the times I shrunk to keep the peace.
- ❖ For the words I swallowed out of fear.
- ❖ For staying when I should have left.

Healing required owning my part in my story, not rewriting it.

And it required seeing myself not as the broken pieces of my past but as the empowered creator of my future.

The Hardest One to Forgive Is Often Ourselves

As we grow and heal, we often look back at earlier versions of ourselves with judgment. We see the choices we made, the people we stayed with, the things we allowed—and we may feel shame, guilt, or regret. But the truth is this: we cannot live in self-love while holding resentment toward ourselves.

You did the best you could with what you knew at the time. And even in the moments when you knew better but still didn't act differently, it may have been because you weren't ready. Readiness is a part of healing. And healing takes time.

Forgiving yourself is a radical act of compassion. It means holding your past self with tenderness, not punishment. It means recognizing your growth and honoring how far you've come. You don't owe yourself perfection. You owe yourself grace.

Practices in Forgiveness

- ❖ When you are angry at someone or a situation. Write out all of your emotions, thoughts, and feelings about it. Let it be honest, unfiltered, and real. No one will ever see it so put it all out there on paper. When you are done, you can do these three things or follow your intuition.
    - ➢ 1. Take a black marker angrily coloring all over it marking it all up as deep hard as you want. Really, let the paper have it!
    - ➢ 2. Tear the paper up, putting all your anger and frustration into it. I mean really obliterate the paper and the emotion. Bonus - put it on the ground and jump up and down on it.
    - ➢ 3. After tearing it up, if you want, safely burn it. As you watch it burn and see the smoke float away in the sky, visualize letting go. Letting go of all the pain, hurt, anger, all the emotions.
- ❖ To forgive yourself. While looking in the mirror, place a hand over your heart and speak aloud:
    - ➢ "I forgive you for (insert what you are harboring) and I love you. Repeat this as many times as needed. Let the words sink in.

- ➤ Trigger warning: this can be a very emotional experience. Give yourself space and time to do it and process all the emotions that come up.

- ❖ When emotions of anger or hurt continue to pop up, take a deep breath, breathing in love and imagine releasing the emotions that need to be released. When you feel it is released, imagine wrapping the person or the situation in love and letting it go. You can even say to yourself: "This is no longer mine to carry. I let it go in love!"

Forgiveness Is a Journey

Forgiveness doesn't always happen all at once. Sometimes it comes in waves. Sometimes, it returns in layers. That's okay. Keep showing up. Keep choosing to let go of what no longer serves you.

Forgiveness is not a weakness. It is liberation. It creates space for peace, joy, and healing where pain once lived.

You deserve to feel light again. You deserve to be free.

You deserve to live in light and love!

Affirmations

- ❖ I choose to let go of what no longer serves me.
- ❖ I am allowed to release anger and reclaim peace.
- ❖ Forgiveness sets me free.
- ❖ I offer myself compassion for all I did not yet know.
- ❖ I can honor my pain without carrying it forever.
- ❖ Each breath is a chance to soften and surrender.

- ❖ I forgive others not to excuse their actions but to free my soul.
- ❖ I am no longer bound by the past—I am creating a new future.
- ❖ I hold space for healing, even when it takes time.
- ❖ I deserve to live with a light and open heart.

Journal Prompts:

1. What pain or resentment am I still holding onto that feels heavy in my body?
2. What would it feel like to forgive—not for them, but for me?
3. What parts of my past self do I take responsibility for?
4. What parts of my past do I need to offer compassion to?
5. In what ways have I withheld forgiveness from myself?
6. What beliefs about forgiveness do I carry, and are they helping or harming me?
7. If I were to release this hurt, what could open up in its place?
8. What rituals or actions help me embody the energy of release?
9. How does my body feel when I think about forgiveness? What needs attention?
10. What would my life look like if I truly forgave myself and others?
11. What support do I need in order to practice forgiveness more fully?

PART - III

Embodiment & Expansion

"To know oneself is to be rooted in being, instead of lost in your mind."

—Eckhart Tolle

Throughout this book, I've shared my heart, my lessons, and the many ways we can gently return to our true selves—the selves we were before life's hardships pulled us away from connection, purpose, peace, and self-love.

This final section is devoted to supportive practices—simple, nurturing ways to continue your healing journey and help sustain the growth you've already begun. Healing is not a straight line; it is a living, breathing journey of ups and downs, ebb and flow. It's a lifestyle rooted in self-love and self-compassion, leading you closer to the peace and presence that is your birthright.

What you'll find here are not rigid formulas or strict routines. Instead, these are invitations—suggestions to support you when you need them and tools you can reach for in the seasons that call for them.

Always, always listen to your body, your soul, and your Spirit. You are your own best guide. Trust yourself to choose what feels right, and allow yourself to leave behind what no longer serves you.

There will be days when a practice feels like exactly what you need—and days when it doesn't. That's okay. Healing is not about doing everything "right." It's about honoring what you need in each moment. It's about remembering that you are a human being, not a human doing.

Give yourself grace. Offer yourself patience. Wrap yourself in love.

And know that with every breath, every choice toward presence and compassion, you are coming home to yourself.

Welcome to the sacred path of embodiment and expansion. You are ready.

CHAPTER 13

Supportive Practices for Growth - Daily Routines That Anchor You

"Embodiment is the last step of transformation—when the lesson becomes lived wisdom."

— *Kimberly Ann Johnson*

Healing isn't something that happens in a single moment—it's something we live into, day by day, choice by choice. And the most powerful shifts often come not from dramatic breakthroughs but from consistent, loving practices that support your nervous system, your spirit, and your growth.

A Lesson from Spirit

In the early days of my healing and self-care journey, I was still learning what it truly meant to support myself in healthy ways. At the time, I was working in the Mental Health Crisis Unit inside a prison, treating clients who were suicidal, gravely disabled, or homicidal. It was intense, emotional work—and on one particular day, it all became too much. Without going into details, by the end of my shift, I was in tears. I felt angry, frustrated, overwhelmed, and heartbroken.

Seeing my distress, the psychiatrist on duty jokingly scribbled me a "prescription" for a bottle of wine. I laughed, grateful for the comic relief, and thought, Perfect—thank you for the excuse! I'm buying a bottle on my way home.

As I drove home, I decided that wine wasn't enough—I was also going to grab some junk food, skip yoga, and spend the night mindlessly eating and drinking my emotions away. I knew it wasn't healthy, but after such a brutal day, I convinced myself I deserved it.

Yet as I drove, Spirit kept gently nudging me: You don't need wine. You don't need junk food. You need yoga. You need meditation.

I argued with that voice for the entire 45-minute drive. I've earned this. I need comfort, not another "lesson." I was determined to ignore the nudge and do things my way.

But when I pulled into town, I discovered the power was out. The CVS I planned to stop at was closed. I drove to three more stores—every one of them dark and locked up. Frustrated, I gave up and went home.

With no other options, I rolled out my mat and did my yoga and meditation practice by candlelight. Then I made a simple salad for dinner. As I sat there eating quietly, Spirit's gentle voice returned: How do you feel now?

The answer was undeniable: I felt 100 times better—peaceful, clear, and grounded.

Spirit asked, And how would you have felt if you'd followed your original plan?

I smiled sadly, knowing the truth. I would have felt terrible—bloated, foggy, disconnected, and disappointed in myself.

As I finished my salad, the power came back on—almost as if Spirit was saying, Well done. You chose to nourish yourself, not numb yourself.

That night taught me a powerful lesson: the comforts we crave in hard moments are often the very things that deepen our pain. True healing sometimes requires us to choose what nurtures our soul, not what soothes our wounds temporarily.

I see this pattern with clients all the time. They know what supports them—mindfulness, movement, nourishing food, connection. But when life gets overwhelming, it's so easy to slip back into old, familiar habits that offer short-term relief but long-term hurt.

As you move through your own healing journey, remember this: When life gets hard, listen to Spirit.

Choose the practices that nourish your wellness, not the old habits that drain it.

Sit with the discomfort instead of distracting from it.

Train your mind and body to grow through presence, not avoidance.

There is real, lasting growth in honoring your needs with love, discipline, and devotion.

There is real peace in choosing yourself again and again.

Taking care of yourself is the most important thing you can do! If you don't take care of yourself, you cannot take care of others! Start where you can and be as consistent as you can, but do it from a place of self-love and nourishment!

Consistency doesn't mean doing things perfectly—it means gently returning to what supports you again and again.

Food as Medicine

The Sacred Link Between Gut and Mind

Our bodies hold ancient wisdom, and nowhere is that more clear than in the connection between our gut and our mind. Modern science is finally catching up to what holistic traditions have known for centuries: the gut is not just where we digest food—it is where we process emotion, intuition, and healing. Researchers now call the gut our "second brain," recognizing that it produces over 90% of the body's serotonin and plays a crucial role in emotional well-being. When our gut is out of balance— through stress, processed foods, environmental toxins, or long-held emotional pain—our minds and hearts feel it deeply. Symptoms like anxiety, depression, mood swings, and chronic fatigue often have roots in gut health. Tending to your gut is an act of sacred self-care. Choosing nourishing foods, slowing down, breathing deeply, and living mindfully aren't just physical acts—they are spiritual ones, helping your inner and outer worlds come back into harmony. Healing begins deep within, and as we heal the gut, we create fertile ground for joy, peace, and vibrant living to grow.

Whenever possible:

- ❖ Avoid processed foods, dyes, chemicals, and excessive sugar.
- ❖ Eat the rainbow of organic fruits and vegetables (preferably locally grown).
- ❖ Choose organic grass-fed meats, wild-caught fish, and pasture or local farm-raised eggs.
- ❖ Speak love and healing into your food as you prepare it.
- ❖ Eat slowly and mindfully, savoring the nourishment.

Nourishment Over Numbing

Think of food not as punishment or reward but as sacred fuel. Your body is worthy of nourishment.

I generally follow the 90/10 rule: 90% of what I eat is clean, organic, whole foods, and 10% is whatever I want. This approach keeps me grounded in balance rather than caught up in rigid rules. When eating becomes about strict "shoulds" and "should nots," we lose sight of the true purpose— nourishing and honoring our bodies with love. Allowing small, intentional indulgences without guilt helps me stay connected to self-compassion rather than falling into cycles of shame.

However, it's important to stay mindful of your patterns around food. If you notice you can't stop once you start splurging, take a closer look. When do you crave sugar? When do you crave processed or comfort foods? What emotions or stresses tend to trigger those cravings?

As I shared earlier, I often catch myself wanting to numb through food when difficult emotions surface. When those urges strike, I pause and ask: What am I really feeling? What needs attention or care right now?

In everything we do, it's important to recognize when we're seeking escape instead of healing.

Remember: you have to feel it to heal it.

Even though that brownie tastes delicious, it won't mend a broken heart. Only love, presence, and self-compassion can do that.

Honor yourself by choosing nourishment—not just for your body, but for your soul.

THE SACRED ART OF SLEEP — REST AS A RADICAL ACT OF HEALING

> "Sleep is the golden chain that ties health and our bodies together."
>
> — *Thomas Dekker*

We live in a world that glorifies productivity, hustle, and pushing through exhaustion. We wear busyness like a badge of honor, often ignoring the quiet, pleading messages from our body and soul asking us to slow down.

But the truth is: Sleep is not a luxury. Sleep is a sacred, biological need. It is one of the most powerful healing medicines available to us— completely free, naturally built-in, and utterly essential.

When we honor sleep, we honor life itself.

Why Sleep Matters So Much

During sleep, your body undergoes deep restoration. It's not just "rest"—it's active, essential healing:

- ❖ Your brain cleanses itself of toxins.
- ❖ Your nervous system resets and repairs.

- ❖ Your muscles, tissues, and cells regenerate.
- ❖ Your emotional brain processes experiences and integrates memories.
- ❖ Your hormones balance and recalibrate.

Without enough sleep, every system in your body suffers. Your immune system weakens. Your emotions become harder to regulate. Your ability to focus, connect, and even heal physically diminishes. Over time, chronic sleep deprivation has been linked to increased rates of anxiety, depression, autoimmune diseases, and even heart disease.

Sleep is your body's nightly chance to heal, reset, and prepare for the blessings of a new day.

New Research: Women Need More Sleep Than Men

Recent studies have revealed something fascinating and important:

Women actually need more sleep than men.

While the general recommendation for adults has long been 7–9 hours, newer research suggests that women, due to the complexity of their hormonal cycles and brain structure, thrive with closer to 9–10 hours of sleep per night.

Women's brains are wired for multitasking, emotional processing, and relational energy—which all require deeper and longer recovery times during sleep. Additionally, hormonal shifts across the menstrual cycle, pregnancy, perimenopause, and menopause put extra demands on the nervous system and body.

Lack of sufficient sleep in women has been linked to increased emotional dysregulation, worsened anxiety and depression symptoms, more intense hormonal imbalances, and slower physical recovery.

If you're a woman reading this: You are not lazy for needing more sleep. You are not weak for needing rest. You are biologically designed to heal deeply through sleep.

Allowing yourself 9–10 hours of sleep (or at least more than 8) is an act of sacred self-care.

Signs You're Not Getting Enough Sleep

- ❖ Feeling emotionally reactive or weepy
- ❖ Brain fog, forgetfulness, or difficulty concentrating
- ❖ Increased anxiety or irritability
- ❖ Craving sugar, caffeine, or processed foods
- ❖ Feeling wired but tired at night
- ❖ Waking up unrefreshed even after sleeping
- ❖ Increased sensitivity to stress

If you notice these patterns, it's your body lovingly asking for more rest, not more stimulation.

How to Support Deeper, More Restorative Sleep

Here are simple, soul-supportive practices to help you create a nourishing sleep routine:

1. **Honor Your Bedtime**

   Go to bed earlier than you think you need to. Many of us push through natural tiredness cues, catching a "second wind" that makes falling asleep harder. Try setting a gentle bedtime ritual 30–60 minutes before sleep to help your body wind down.

2. **Limit Screens and Blue Light**

   Blue light from phones, TVs, and computers tricks your brain into thinking it's daytime. Turn off electronics at least an hour before bed, or use blue- light-blocking glasses to help your brain naturally produce melatonin (your sleep hormone).

3. **Create a Calm Sleep Environment**

   Make your bedroom a sanctuary for sleep:

   - ❖ Cool, dark, and quiet
   - ❖ Free of clutter
   - ❖ Soft, cozy bedding
   - ❖ Essential oils like lavender or chamomile
   - ❖ White noise machines or soft nature sounds, if needed

Your nervous system will associate this space with peace and rest.

4. **Support Your Circadian Rhythm**

   Get outside in natural sunlight during the day, especially in the morning. Even 10 minutes helps regulate your body's internal clock and supports nighttime melatonin production.

5. **Mind Your Evening Rituals**

   Avoid heavy meals, caffeine, or intense exercise too close to bedtime. Instead, opt for soothing activities:

- ❖ Stretching or gentle yoga
- ❖ Herbal tea (like chamomile, lemon balm, or passionflower)
- ❖ Journaling gratitudes or reflections
- ❖ Listening to calming music or meditation

6. **Use Breathwork or Guided Meditation**

    If your mind races at night, use simple breathwork (like a 4-7-8 breathing pattern) or guided sleep meditations to relax your nervous system and drift peacefully into sleep.

Sleep as a Spiritual Practice

Sleep is not laziness. Sleep is not a weakness.

Sleep is a sacred practice of trust.

Every time you lay your head down, you are practicing surrender. You are affirming that life will continue even when you are not "doing." You are trusting your body to heal, your mind to sort, and Spirit to watch over you.

Each night, let yourself be loved by the universe as you sleep. Allow sleep to be a doorway into healing, restoration, and a deeper connection to yourself.

You deserve deep, nourishing rest—not just occasionally, but daily.

Give yourself permission to create a life where sleep is honored. Let sleep be part of your healing.

Let sleep be a radical act of self-love.

Meditation Sets the Tone for Your Life

As mentioned earlier in this book, meditation is not just a practice — it's a way of setting the tone for your entire life. Even a few minutes a day can create powerful shifts in your mind, body, and spirit. Meditation calms the nervous system, clears mental clutter, helps regulate emotions, and reconnects you with your inner truth. It's not about forcing your mind to be silent — it's about building a relationship with yourself through presence and compassion. When you begin your day rooted in stillness and awareness, you carry that energy with you into everything you do.

Meditation is one of the most powerful tools you can use to create a life of intention, peace, and authentic joy.

The Healing Power of Breathwork

Breath is life. In yogic traditions, it's understood that our breath carries prana—the vital life force that animates every cell, every thought, every emotion. Breath isn't just air moving in and out of the lungs; it's the sacred bridge between body, mind, and spirit.

When we breathe deeply and consciously, we invite fresh prana into our system, helping to cleanse the blood, oxygenate our cells, and flush out toxins that build up from stress, poor diet, and emotional suppression.

Shallow, rapid breathing—a hallmark of anxiety and trauma—keeps us stuck in survival mode. It signals to the body that danger is near, keeping us tense, reactive, and exhausted.

Through intentional breathwork, we disrupt that cycle. We signal safety to the nervous system. We slow down the heart rate. We move stagnant energy that might otherwise stay trapped in the body as anxiety, sadness, or even physical pain.

Breathwork can also be a profound tool for emotional release. Many times, the feelings we've tucked away—grief, anger, fear—begin to surface as we breathe deeply and consciously. This is not something to fear; it's the body's natural way of clearing out what no longer serves us. With each inhale, we draw in life, hope, and healing. With each exhale, we release old patterns, old pain, and old stories.

Breath is our anchor. It is the easiest, most accessible, and most powerful tool we have to return to ourselves—again and again.

When you breathe with intention, you remind your entire being:

I am here. I am alive. I am safe. I am healing.

The Transformative Power of Yoga

Yoga is far more than stretching or physical fitness—it is a sacred practice of union: body, mind, breath, and spirit working together in harmony. In its true essence, yoga means "to yoke" or "to unite," bringing us back to wholeness when life, trauma, and stress have pulled us apart.

Through conscious movement, breath, and mindfulness, yoga creates a pathway for healing. As we move through poses, we increase circulation, nourish our organs, strengthen our muscles, and create greater flexibility not only in the body but also in the heart and mind. On a deeper level, yoga invites us to listen—to feel where tension, grief, fear, or anger may be stored. Our bodies hold emotions like memories written into our muscles and fascia. With each mindful movement, we create the opportunity to release what has been trapped inside, sometimes for years.

Practicing yoga helps regulate the nervous system, supporting a shift from fight-or-flight into rest and healing. It balances the energy centers of the body (chakras), aligns the spine—the body's communication highway—and cultivates presence in the now, where true transformation happens.

Yoga teaches us to be with ourselves, even when discomfort arises. It strengthens not just the physical body but also our inner resilience, patience, and compassion. It offers the gift of coming home—to a body that is no longer the battleground of stress and trauma but a sanctuary of peace, power, and love.

Every time you step onto your mat, you send a powerful message to your entire being: *I am worthy of healing. I am reconnecting. I am returning to myself.*

The Healing Power of Journaling

Journaling is more than simply putting words on a page—it is a profound act of self-connection and emotional alchemy. When we give our thoughts and feelings a voice through writing, we create space for clarity, healing, and transformation.

Our emotions and experiences live within us like unwritten stories. Left unspoken, they can swirl inside, creating confusion, anxiety, or even physical pain. Journaling offers a sacred container where we can release those emotions safely—where nothing is judged and everything is welcome. As we write, we unearth hidden fears, buried hopes, and forgotten dreams. We begin to see ourselves more clearly, witnessing both the parts that ache and the parts that long to heal.

Writing also activates a unique connection between the heart and the mind. By translating inner experience into language, we invite understanding, integration, and growth. Journaling helps cleanse the emotional body, similar to how breathwork cleanses the blood—it moves stagnant energy out of hiding and into the light.

Through this simple but powerful practice, we learn to listen more deeply to ourselves. We honor the truths we carry. We offer compassion to the parts that are hurting.

Each page becomes a stepping stone back to our own wholeness.

Every time you sit down with your journal, you affirm:

My voice matters. My healing matters. My story is sacred.

The Power of Reading Inspirational and Healing Texts

Recognizing the importance of nourishing not just the body but the mind and spirit, is a crucial part of any healing journey. If your goal is personal growth, transformation, or simply living more intentionally, immersing yourself in inspirational and supportive texts can be one of the most powerful tools you have. It has been one of the foundations of my healing journey for years—and continues to be a source of light, guidance, and encouragement through every season of life.

Reading healing-focused books, poetry, or sacred wisdom is like watering the soil of your soul. These texts remind you of who you truly are when life tries to make you forget. They offer new perspectives, uplift your spirit on hard days, and gently challenge the old beliefs that no longer serve your highest good. The right words can open doorways in the heart, helping you access deeper layers of insight, compassion, and resilience.

When we surround ourselves with wisdom—whether ancient teachings, mindful living books, or the personal stories of others who have walked the path of healing—we begin to rewire our inner landscape. These words become seeds planted in our consciousness, slowly growing into new thoughts, new patterns, and new ways of being.

Even just a few minutes a day spent with a healing book can shift your energy, lift your perspective, and anchor you back into your truth. Let reading become a sacred part of your self-care—an act of devotion to your growth, your spirit, and your limitless potential.

Make Life a Ritual

There is something truly magical about slowing down and moving through life with intention. I have a dear friend who embodies this beautifully.

Watching her move through her day is like watching a sacred ceremony unfold. When she sets up her yoga mat, it's not rushed—it's an act of devotion. When she wanders her property to collect wildflowers, she does so with care, attention, and awe, creating stunning arrangements that feel like offerings to life itself. Every action she takes is mindful, infused with presence and reverence.

Witnessing her changed something in me. It opened my eyes to how often I had been rushing—even through things I loved. I realized how much beauty I was missing by moving too fast. Since then, I've made it a practice to create rituals out of the ordinary moments. I speak lovingly to my garden while I water it. I say affirmations as I care for my skin. I take time to truly savor my meals rather than hurrying through them between sessions.

It's not the task itself that matters—it's the energy you bring to it. When you slow down and move through life with presence, you raise your vibration.

Simple moments become sacred. Ordinary days become extraordinary. Life feels more magical, more peaceful, more aligned.

The act of slowing down isn't just romantic or spiritual—it's also deeply healing for your nervous system. When you invite ritual into your daily life, you send a powerful message to your body and spirit: "We are safe. We are connected. We are alive to the beauty of this moment."

A Gentle Reminder: Nourishing Yourself with Love

Throughout this chapter, we've explored a variety of nourishing practices—breathwork, yoga, journaling, meditation, mindful eating, deep sleep, tending to gut health, and the powerful art of slowing down and creating ritual in everyday life. Each of these practices is a beautiful way to honor your body, mind, and spirit.

But remember: *this is not about perfection*.

It's about listening inward, honoring your intuition, and choosing what feels most supportive for you right now. Healing is not a race, and self-care is not another item on your to-do list. It's an act of love—a way of coming home to yourself, one small step at a time.

Start where you are. Pick one practice that calls to you and let it anchor you in self-love. Add more as you feel ready or as your body whispers that it needs more nourishment. Let your journey be intuitive, fluid, and kind.

And if you find yourself slipping into old habits or falling off track, don't judge yourself. Simply notice, breathe, and gently return to what nurtures you. Healing happens in the return. It's the ongoing commitment to care for yourself with compassion that creates lasting transformation.

You are worthy of a life filled with care, presence, and love—and these practices are simply tools to help you remember that truth.

As we move into the next chapter, we'll take a closer look at one of the most important systems we must support on the healing journey: the nervous system. Understanding how it shapes our reactions, emotions, and sense of safety will empower you to deepen your healing from the inside out. Let's explore how you can begin to rewire your body for peace, presence, and lasting freedom.

Affirmations

Read these aloud or write them in a place you'll see daily.

- ❖ I ground myself each day through intentional, loving choices.
- ❖ My daily routines are sacred acts of self-devotion.
- ❖ I honor my body by giving it what it needs—nourishment, rest, and presence.
- ❖ I am worthy of creating rituals that support my peace and joy.
- ❖ Small, mindful actions create lasting transformation.
- ❖ I return to myself through breath, rhythm, and intention.
- ❖ My healing is supported by the structure I lovingly create.

Journal Prompts

1. What does a "supportive daily rhythm" look like to me in this season of life?
2. What small routines or habits already bring me a sense of grounding or peace?
3. In what ways can I turn ordinary tasks into sacred rituals?

4. What would it feel like to approach my mornings or evenings as a ceremony?

5. What has kept me from creating or committing to supportive daily practices in the past—and how can I shift that now?

6. If my body could choose one daily ritual just for itself, what would it ask for?

7. How does my energy shift when I move through the day with intention versus rushing or reacting?

CHAPTER 14

Healing the Nervous System - My Wake-Up Call

"Our nervous system is not just a survival system—it is a map back home to safety, presence, and connection."

— ***Kimberly Ann Johnson***

Recognizing the Wake-Up Call

After my divorce, while still working full-time in the prison system, I found myself completely depleted. No matter how much I slept, I was always tired. My weight kept climbing despite everything I tried. When I finally went to the doctor, lab results showed I had low thyroid function. The doctor prescribed medication and said, "This is just what happens when we live stressful lives. The adrenal system gets burned out. There's nothing you can do but medicate it."

That response shook me. If stress was the problem, there had to be something I could do about my stress. That moment lit a fire in me to understand the nervous system and how to support it—not just mask its cries for help.

That experience was a major turning point for me. It opened my eyes to the reality that true healing isn't just about managing symptoms — it's about understanding and supporting the systems that keep us alive. Our nervous system holds the key to so much of how we experience life: how we react to stress, how we feel emotionally, and how connected we feel to ourselves and the world around us.

That experience was Spirit's wake-up call for me: a reminder that I wasn't meant to live stuck in survival mode. True healing meant more than masking symptoms — it meant reconnecting with the intelligence and wisdom already built into my body.

Your nervous system is your inner compass, your sacred guide. When it's regulated and supported, you feel grounded, clear, and resilient. When it's overwhelmed, everything in life feels heavier and harder.

In the next section, we'll explore how to recognize the different states of your nervous system and begin building a powerful toolkit to help you return to balance whenever life pulls you off center. Your body is not your enemy — it's your greatest ally on this journey home to yourself.

Mapping Nervous System States

The nervous system is your body's communication hub. When it's healthy and balanced, it helps you feel calm, focused, and safe. But when it's overworked, it can get stuck in high-alert or shut-down mode.

Here are the three main states of your autonomic nervous system:

- ❖ Sympathetic (Fight, Flight, or Freeze): You feel anxious, reactive, and overwhelmed.

- ❖ Parasympathetic (Rest and Digest): You feel calm, grounded, and at peace.

- ❖ Dorsal Vagal (Shutdown): You feel numb, disconnected, or depressed.

Many of us live in a chronic state of hypervigilance or shutdown. But with awareness and daily support, the nervous system can shift back into regulation.

Signs of Dysregulation

If your nervous system is struggling, you might notice:

- ❖ Chronic exhaustion or burnout
- ❖ Sleep disturbances
- ❖ Brain fog, memory lapses
- ❖ Panic attacks or persistent anxiety
- ❖ Irritability or emotional numbness
- ❖ Digestive issues or chronic pain
- ❖ Difficulty feeling safe, even in peaceful environments

These are not failures—they're your body waving a red flag. They're signals that your system needs attention, care, and repair.

Rewiring the Body with Somatic Tools

The goal isn't to avoid stress completely—it's to increase your resilience. The more we learn to regulate, the more we can return to peace no matter what's happening around us.

Here are simple tools to support and heal your nervous system:

- ❖ Breathwork:
    - ➤ Try inhaling for 4 counts, holding for 2, and exhaling for 8.
    - ➤ This helps activate your parasympathetic nervous system.

- ❖ Cold Exposure:
    - ➤ Splash cold water on your face or end your shower with 30 seconds of cold.

- ➢ Cold stimulates the vagus nerve, improving resilience.

- ❖ Sound & Vibration:
  - ➢ Humming, chanting, and singing help calm the nervous system.
  - ➢ Listening to binaural beats can promote relaxation.
  - ➢ Attend a sound bath

- ❖ Gentle Movement:
  - ➢ Walk, stretch, sway, or rock your body.
  - ➢ Movement helps discharge stress from the body.
  - ➢ Butterfly taps: hug yourself with each hand on your shoulder alternating tapping each side.

- ❖ Grounding Techniques:
  - ➢ Walk barefoot on the earth, touch trees, or sit in the sun.
  - ➢ Grounding restores presence and connection to the Earth.

- ❖ Somatic Awareness:
  - ➢ Tune into where stress or emotion lives in your body.
  - ➢ Place a hand there and breathe with compassion.

- ❖ Safe Connection:
  - ➢ Eye contact, supportive conversation, and physical touch all tell the

nervous system: "You're safe."

Each of these may seem small, but repeated consistently, they change your inner landscape. You begin to move from chaos to calm, from survival to healing.

A New Way of Living

That doctor was wrong—stress isn't inevitable. It can be healed. Managed. Softened. Transformed.

We cannot avoid hard things. But we can learn to meet them from a place of presence, power, and deep inner peace.

Your nervous system has been fighting for you all along. Now, it's time to give it the support it deserves.

Affirmations

- ❖ I am safe in my body.
- ❖ My nervous system knows how to return to balance.
- ❖ I honor the messages my body gives me.
- ❖ I release urgency and choose peace.
- ❖ I am allowed to rest and receive.
- ❖ I trust my body's wisdom and capacity to heal.
- ❖ I gently return to calm with every breath I take.
- ❖ I am no longer at war with my body—I am in partnership with it.
- ❖ I create space for stillness and healing every day.
- ❖ I am rooted, present, and whole.

Journal Prompts

1. When do I feel most regulated, grounded, or safe in my body?
2. What are some early signs that my nervous system is dysregulated?
3. How have I ignored or overridden my body's cues in the past?
4. What small daily rituals can I begin (or return to) that help me feel more at ease?
5. What does "safety" feel like—emotionally, physically, spiritually?
6. What beliefs do I hold around rest, stillness, or slowing down? Are they serving me?
7. How can I offer more compassion to my body when it's trying to protect me?
8. What would it feel like to fully trust my body's ability to heal?

CHAPTER 15

A New Way of Being — Presence, Surrender, and Integration

"The privilege of a lifetime is to become who you truly are."

— *Carl Jung*

If you've made it here, I want you to pause for a moment and acknowledge something extraordinary:

- ❖ You showed up for yourself.
- ❖ You chose to look inward, feel deeply, heal courageously, and begin the sacred process of transformation.
- ❖ You committed to becoming more mindful, embracing self-love, surrendering control, and walking the path of deep inner healing.

Each chapter offered a different piece of the whole—awareness, presence, shadow work, alignment, trust—and through it all, you remained open to growth. That is something to be proud of.

That's not small. That's not easy. And that's not common. Celebrate yourself today!

The journey you've taken through these chapters was not about perfection—it was about cultivating mindfulness, embracing presence, surrendering to the process, and learning to meet yourself with compassion and curiosity at every step. It was about presence. It was about slowly remembering who you are, what matters to you, and how to align your life with your deepest truth.

Healing Is a Lifelong Journey

Let this be a reminder: there is no final destination. The journey continues, and as life shifts and changes, the tools and lessons in this book will meet you in new ways. Revisit them often. Let this work evolve with you.

You will still have hard days. You will still feel triggered, tired, and overwhelmed. But now, you have tools. You have awareness. You have compassion. You have Spirit.

Healing is not about getting it right. It's about coming home to yourself again and again.

Live With Intention, Move With Grace

Keep building the practices that support you—like your morning breathwork, grounding meditations, mindful movement, and connecting to nature. Let these rituals become your anchors, and allow them to grow and evolve with you. Return to your breath. Return to your body. Return to the earth. Speak love to yourself. Rest when you need it. Take up space when you're ready.

Don't wait until your life is perfect to start living it. Let beauty in now. Let love in now. You are ready, even if your mind tells you otherwise.

Let life become your practice. Let presence become your path. Let peace become your baseline.

A Final Invitation

This book was never meant to be a list of steps or a rigid program. It is a companion you can return to in different seasons of your life, a source of reflection, guidance, and renewed connection whenever you need it. It was a map back to your own wisdom.

My hope is that something in these pages woke up a part of you that you had forgotten. A voice that says:

I deserve to feel good. I am allowed to rest.

I can live in alignment. I am whole.

I am healing. I am enough.

FROM MY HEART TO YOURS

If you're reading this, it means you've made a powerful, conscious choice—to come to this earth, in this lifetime, to heal, to grow, and to rise. You are a brave soul. Some of us came carrying generations of pain and chose the path of deep healing. That takes courage beyond measure.

But Spirit never sends us here alone. We are given support in many forms—through people, messages, synchronicities, and the inner voice that whispers the truth when we're quiet enough to listen. You are not alone. You are divinely loved and deeply cherished.

When life feels heavy, when the path gets blurry, remember how far you've come. Remember that the fire you walk through today is also the fire that forges your strength. The blessings on the other side of that fire are greater than you can imagine.

Be tender with yourself in all things. Allow yourself to rest. Allow yourself to pause. The world will wait. Listen to your intuition—it is sacred and trustworthy, even when quiet. This connection to your inner guidance is a gift, and like any skill, it grows with time, love, and practice.

Even when it feels hard, even when doubt creeps in—you are on the path. Trust that. Let yourself be guided. Let yourself be loved.

Thank you for being here. I'm sending you all the love in the world for your journey.

With deepest gratitude and light,— Kim

ABOUT THE AUTHOR

Kimberly Weimer, LCSW, is a licensed therapist, certified hypnotherapist, meditation teacher, and yoga instructor with over 20 years of experience in the field of holistic mental health. As the founder of The Lotus Healing Center, she integrates evidence-based practices with mindfulness, somatic awareness, and spiritual wisdom to support deep healing and transformation.

Kimberly's work is grounded in the belief that we are not broken—we are becoming. Through her writing, workshops, and private practice, she helps others reclaim their light, regulate their nervous systems, and reconnect with the truth of who they are.

Her own healing journey—through trauma, motherhood, intuition, and spiritual awakening—inspires the sacred guidance offered in this book. She lives on a peaceful homestead in California, where she spends her days gardening, walking with her dogs, and holding space for healing.